DAYS OUT IN LONDON

by Edward Prendeville

Exploring 15 London Neighbourhoods

Days Out in London

Written by Edward Prendeville
Edited by Eve Kershman
Photography by Metro (further image credits see p.314)
Front cover by Malgorzata Larys / Alamy Stock Photo
Design by Susi Koch & Lesley Gilmour
Illustrations by Lesley Gilmour & Hannah Kershman

All rights reserved. No part of this publication may be reproduced, stored in a retrieval system or transmitted in any form or by any means electronic, mechanical, photocopying, recording or otherwise without the prior consent of the publishers and copyright owners. Every effort has been made to ensure the accuracy of this book; however, due to the nature of the subject the publishers cannot accept responsibility for any errors which occur, or their consequences.

First edition published in 2025 by
Metro Publications Ltd
www.metropublications.com

Metro® is a registered trade mark of Associated Newspapers Limited.
The METRO mark is under licence from Associated Newspapers Limited.

Printed and bound in Turkey.
This book is made of certified and controlled material.

© 2025 Metro Publications Ltd
British Library Cataloguing in Publication Data. A catalogue record for this book is available from the British Library.

ISBN 978-1-902910-82-6

The authorised representative in the EEA is:
Thomas Mertenskötter
Donnerstr. 18, 22763 Hamburg, Germany

DAYS OUT IN LONDON

by Edward Prendeville

Flask Walk, see p.72

Contents

CENTRAL
1. Bloomsbury 5
2. Soho 27
3. Barbican 47

NORTH
4. Hampstead 65
5. Stoke Newington 79
6. Islington 99

EAST
7. Hackney 121
8. Shoreditch 141
9. Walthamstow 163

SOUTH
10. Borough & Bermondsey 185
11. Brixton 209
12. Greenwich 227

WEST
13. Notting Hill 249
14. Richmond 267
15. Hammersmith & Chiswick 287

Acknowledgements

I'd like to thank everyone at Metro Publications for their help and support in writing this book. Susi Koch and Andrew Kershman were there every step of the way, from designing the book's pages to providing support and guidance. Andrew also took on the Herculean task of doing most of the photography; his images have helped bring the book to life. Hannah Kershman and Lesley Gilmour deserve special mention, as their expertly made maps have transformed my list of recommendations into a user-friendly, area-coded guide. My editor, Eve Kershman, has also gone to great lengths to spare you, the reader, from tripping up over spelling mistakes and wayward grammar, and turned the book into a far smoother read.

In the time it's taken to research and write this book, I have had the pleasure of visiting a great many London establishments and speaking to their passionate proprietors. Surviving the various pressures of gentrification, the pandemic and the cost-of-living crisis is no small feat, and it has been a privilege to tell their stories. Lastly, my thanks go to all those people I've had chance encounters with that have offered recommendations of their neighbourhood, which have helped make this book a far better portrait of the city we love.

Introduction

London is an ancient city, so old that even the origins of its name remain a mystery. Established by the Romans nearly two millennia ago, it once stood as the largest city in the world, at the heart of the most powerful empire in history. Today, it remains among the most expansive, wealthy, influential, and visited cities on the planet. This enduring legacy is rooted in London's remarkable ability to reinvent itself. Long-standing landmarks and local businesses can disappear overnight, only to be replaced by contemporary innovations, creating a city where the old and new stand cheek by jowl.

Contrary to Dr Johnson's adage, it's easy to grow tired of London. The city can become little more than a crowded commute, an uninspired lunch near work, and the occasional weekend visit to a pub or museum. But there is so much more to discover, and that's where this guide comes in. Whether you are a resident or a visitor, this book will help you explore London beyond a hastily Googled itinerary. How? By delving into the diverse neighbourhoods that span the capital, from its historic centre to its furthest corners in the north, east, south, and west.

London is a patchwork of villages, each with a unique past and character. These areas have evolved through the centuries, absorbing the changes of each era while retaining an underlying identity. At first glance, they don't seem to have much of the British village we romanticise in art and literature. But if you look closely, the spirit of the village is still alive in every neighbourhood. And once-rural features and common land have been transformed into many of the city's parks and gardens, making London a surprisingly green place to enjoy.

This book will be your guide to the lesser known but fascinating corners of London. Packed with insider tips, you'll discover secluded and serene sections of Hampstead Heath, learn where to hang out in Hackney, what to spot along Hammersmith's picturesque stretch of the Thames, and why Greenwich offers much more than its remarkable museums. London has never been so accessible, with free activities and fast transport links making it easier than ever to explore.

Fifteen diverse neighbourhoods are featured, with user-friendly maps and detailed reviews of local museums and galleries, the best shopping spots, places to eat and green spaces to walk and relax in – making each area a perfect destination for a day out in London. I hope you enjoy this books as much as I have enjoyed researching it and we look forward to hearing how you get on.

Edward Prendeville
info@metropublications.com

Central

Bloomsbury
Soho
Barbican

Bloomsbury

Bloomsbury is a picture postcard of London. Between the Regency era architecture, the unparalleled collection at the British Museum and the plaques and former homes of the areas famous past residents, there is so much to get lost in. Initially a rural parish attached to St Giles Hospital, and for many centuries an afterthought of its aristocratic owners, things really took off in the 18th century under the Dukes of Bedford and Russell family, who financed the building of the many Georgian townhouses and public squares that characterise the built environment here. Today, Bloomsbury still contains the highest proportion of listed buildings and monuments in the capital. Many house some of the country's most important institutions – the University of London's various member universities, as well as the Royal Academy of Dramatic Art (RADA) and Architectural Association. It's little wonder so many historical figures, from the Bloomsbury Group to the Pre-Raphaelite Brotherhood, chose to call this neighbourhood home. If you want to retrace their steps, you'll find this easy to do – the area is especially suited to pedestrians and blue plaques are to be spotted everywhere. However, every trip here should include the main event – the British Museum. This can easily take all day, but if you're left with time and energy afterwards, do peruse the smaller museums and many bookshops in the surrounding streets. Lamb's Conduit Street will easily satisfy your shopping and eating needs, and if you've got kids in tow then Coram's Fields at the northern end is sure to occupy their energy. Before you leave, do see one of the many public park squares, which are surely Bloomsbury's most charming and unique feature.

BLOOMSBURY

1. British Museum
2. Brunei Gallery SOAS
3. Charles Dickens Museum
4. Foundling Museum
5. Grant Museum of Zoology
6. Jeremy Bentham's Auto-Icon
7. The Wellcome Trust & Collection
8. Brunswick Centre
9. Camera Museum
10. Condor Cycles
11. London Review Bookshop
12. Pentreath & Hall
13. Present & Correct
14. Skoob Books
15. Waterstones Gower Street
16. Andrew's Restaurant
17. Bloomsbury Farmers Market
18. Ciao Bella
19. The Duke
20. The Lamb
21. Noble Rot
22. Otto's
23. Brunswick Square Gardens
24. Coram's Fields
25. Gordon Square
26. St George's Gardens
27. Russell Square
28. Tavistock Square

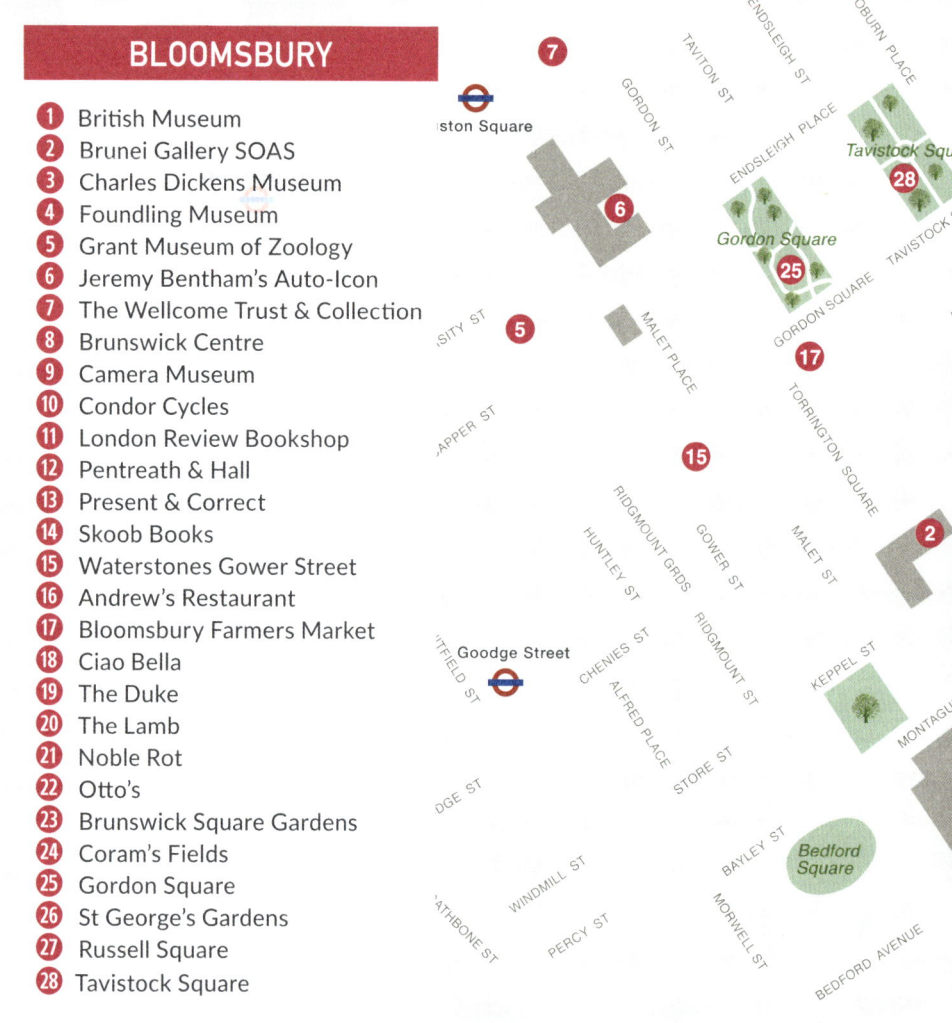

Visit

❶ British Museum
The objective record in objects

For more than six million visitors annually, many good days out start at the British Museum. The world's first public national museum is integral to school trips, but flocks of adults also attend daily to admire the permanent collection of some eight million artefacts – the largest and most comprehensive of its kind. Too expansive and diverse to hope to cover in a day, the British Museum calls for return visits, but there are both free introductory tours, lasting 30-40 minutes, or multilingual multimedia guides, for those wishing to cover the highlights. The day starts in the much-photographed Norman Foster-built Great Court. A spiralling, vast ceiling covers the atrium where the café, restaurant & bookshops reside. The Egyptian galleries tend to be the most popular attraction, with crowds regularly visiting the mummies they house, whilst the Japanese and ethnographic collections offer a quieter experience that is every bit as awe-inspiring. However, if you only have the one day to see the British Museum's sights, prioritise the temporary exhibitions, which are always worth the additional expense or concentrate on a particular period, rather than try to see too much in a single visit. This national collection will always reward numerous visits, so take your time and enjoy the experience.
Great Russell Street, WC1B 3DG;
020 7323 8299; britishmuseum.org

❷ Brunei Gallery SOAS
London's slice of Zen life

Though belonging to the School of Oriental and African Studies, the Brunei Gallery is open to the public as a cornerstone of Museum Mile. What starts as a series of exhibitions on Asian, African and Middle Eastern culture progresses onto a Zen roof garden that remains one of London's most tranquil places. Collections cover topics from Namibian musical history to Japanese lacquer work and are as much a student resource as public facility for exploring cultures all too often overlooked.
Thornhaugh Street, Russell Square, WC1H 0XG;
020 7898 4915; soas.ac.uk

❸ Charles Dickens Museum
Home of the great novelist

Few Londoners are as eminent as Dickens, whose vision of the capital is synonymous with the macabre, dystopian and comic. Get to know the great man by visiting the Georgian townhouse he once called home. Since 1925 it has showcased manuscripts, letters and rare editions, in thematically reproduced rooms. Occasional candlelit tours are a hit with all age groups, while a garden café offers welcome pause from the busy narrative of this prodigious talent. Doughty Street is a little off the busy thoroughfares of Bloomsbury, but for lovers of Dickens, this museum is worth seeking out.
48-49 Doughty Street, WC1N 2LX;
020 7405 2127; dickensmuseum.com

❹ The Foundling Museum
Thomas Coram's philanthropic treasure

This unique museum tells the story of Thomas Coram and the children's hospital and public gallery he founded in 1739. Coram's philanthropy was triggered by the many babies abandoned in the capital by destitute mothers at the time. One of the most moving exhibits is the collection of tokens left with the foundlings. The Foundling Hospital attracted artistic and royal patronage and acquired a considerable art collection, becoming Britain's first public gallery including works by Hogarth, Ramsay and Reynolds. The museum that now stands on the old site of the hospital is a surprising hidden gem and one well worth exploring.

93 Guildford Street, WC1 1DN & 40 Brunswick Square, WC1N 1AZ; foundlingmuseum.org.uk

❺ Grant Museum of Zoology
Natural history's most shocking specimens

You'll find the weird, wonderful and downright disturbing at UCL's Grant Museum of Zoology, with the jar of moles taking top prize. The 68,000 specimens comprise the last London university zoological collection. On display are examples of extinct animals like Dodo bones and Quagga skins, but it's the grizzly jarred specimens and skeletons that catch the eye. Bisected primate craniums will make your head hurt, while a floating Penis Worm raises many unanswered questions. A personal favourite is the Micrarium – a backlit cave of 2300 microscope slides showcasing the diversity of minute animal life – it's the most wondrous way for all ages to be enthused by the 95% of known species that happen to be smaller than your thumb. Free of charge and without the usual queues of Kensington's Natural History Museum, go to the Grant collection for your zoological fix instead.

Rockefeller Building, 21 University Street, WC1E 6DE; ucl.ac.uk

❻ Jeremy Bentham's Auto-Icon
London's original oddity

In a glass-fronted case at the end of UCL's south cloisters sits Jeremy Bentham's skeleton, hidden under a wax model head and padded clothing. The founder of utilitarianism and polymath's real head, mummified and conserved in a bell jar, sits in a wooden safe at the university's institute of archaeology. This auto-icon is Bentham's alternative to funerals, which he saw as socially and medically problematic, and to marble statues, which were costly. He wanted a place where his admirers could gather, and persuaded a doctor friend to dissect him (after his passing) in front of an audience and then preserve his remains. The doctor kept the body at his own dinner table for 18 years until his wife objected. This makes Bentham probably the first person to donate his body to medical research. As for his real head, after an initial embalming went wrong, it is now only brought out at occasional university meetings and events. One last point of trivia: the heads, real and wax, have each been kidnapped by rival King's College students for a ransom then paid to charity.

Gower Street, WC1E 6BT; ucl.ac.uk

❼ The Wellcome Trust & Collection
Museum dedicated to medicine and health

A swank foyer, airy café and arty bookshop set the scene for this museum's lingering appeal. The Trust's collection of medical antiquities should provide adequate distraction. A modern display in the Medicine Man gallery showcases Henry Wellcome's own macabre cabinet of curiosities, from which the entire collection has grown. The real star of the show is the new Being Human gallery. Designed by Turner Prize-winning collective Assemble, it showcases all that is current in our understandings of health, covering research and artwork exploring genetics, mind and body, infection and most significantly, environmental breakdown. This exhibition space is one of the most interactive and eye-catching in London. For many, however, the Reading Room is still where an hour or two spare is best spent – armchairs and beanbags line the walls of an inspiring, plush space alongside a collection of several thousand books. In addition, all exhibitions and spaces are free and open to the public.

183-193 Euston Road, NW1 2BE;
wellcome.ac.uk

Shop

⑧ Brunswick Centre
Once-maligned modernist masterpiece
This Jenga stack of residential and retail space is the pride and joy of Bloomsbury. The 1960s ziggurat design has earned it Grade II status. Inside are plenty of chain stores and cafés, amongst which are also a couple of standout independents. However, what many come for is one of London's most loved cinemas. Once called The Renoir, and now operating under the name Curzon Bloomsbury, it retains its architectural charm and focus on art house films. Follow up a visit here with an al fresco dinner to see how the after-dark lights make this place come to life.
1 Byng Place, WC1N 1BS;
brunswick.co.uk

⑨ Camera Museum
Tea, cake and twin-lens reflexes
What started life 20 years ago as a café run by two brothers with a budding side passion for cameras has evolved and expanded into a go-to dealership and repair service for high-end photography brands – think Hasselblad and Rolleiflex. What's more, it doubles as a museum exhibiting a timeline of cameras and their development from the 1800s to today's digital era. Admission is £1 for adults and free for under-10s.
44 Museum Street, WC1A 1LY;
cameramuseum.uk

⑩ Condor Cycles
London's most famous bike shop
Established in 1948 by Monty Young, this bespoke bike specialist is trusted by Olympians, celebrities and everyday enthusiasts. But if a £10,000 bike isn't on your radar, they have frames from other trusted manufacturers and their stock of components is second to none in the city, providing an alternative way to affordably optimise your setup. A popular servicing workshop has 70 years' experience and is always willing to offer advice. Cyclists can also smarten up their image with a beautiful selection of jerseys, jackets and caps. Even if you're not in the market for new stuff, Condor is always worth a visit just to admire the bikes on display.
49-53 Grays Inn Rd, WC1X 8PP;
condorcycles.com

⑪ London Review Bookshop
Bolthole for a new Bloomsbury Set
The London Review of Books, is a renowned literary publication, that has its own bookshop in the heart of Bloomsbury. The shop's interior is cosy and the diversity of stocked titles is impressive, with 20,000 or so ranging from classics to emergent fiction, academic and popular non-fiction texts, cookery and children's books galore. Weekly literary events, ranging from book signings to poetry recitals means there's something for everyone here.
14-16 Bury Place, WC1A 2JL;
londonreviewbookshop.co.uk

Bloomsbury - Shop

⓬ Pentreath & Hall
Antique interiors reimagined
The couple behind this shop have channelled backgrounds in architecture, interior design and decorative art into their stores. They exhibit a miscellany of British objects for the home. The stock ranges from soft furnishing to stationery and furniture too, with a focus on traditional and antique styles, but with a fresh breath of life and colour. Watch out for the eye-catching, old-fashioned lilac shop front when out gift hunting down Lambs Conduit.
17 Rugby Street, W1CN 3QT;
57 Lamb's Conduit Street, WC1N 3NB;
pentreath-hall.com

⓭ Present & Correct
The ultimate stationery shop
The ephemera of office organisation might sound a boring aspect of modern living, but this little shop in the heart of Bloomsbury turns it into an art form. Expect to find stylish Italian staplers, heavy duty tape dispensers and a bewildering range of pens and pencils. If you're looking for gift ideas for the office geek in your life this beautifully decorated white cube of a shop is a definite first stop. It's a great place to peruse on a day out in Bloomsbury and you're sure to emerge with something special whether it's airmail string, a simple Rollbahn notebook or 70s style office wall clock.
12 Bury Place, W1CN 3QT;
presentandcorrect.com

⑭ Skoob Books
Palindromic literary palace
A highlight of The Brunswick Centre, Skoob is a sanctuary for second-hand academic books – they boast the broadest selection in London. The jumble of shelves, for many a fairy tale setting, carry an uncatalogued sprawl of 55,000 works, that regularly rotate with the over 1,000,000 books they warehouse. Across fiction and non-fiction, topics cover Philosophy, Psychology, Modern Literature, Art, History, Politics, Economics, Classics, and the Sciences. Other items for sale include organic cotton tote bags and classic book cover posters.
66 Brunswick Square, WC1N 1AE;
skoob.com

⑮ Waterstones Gower Street
Chain bookshop's magnum opus
Surrounded by UCL's campus is Europe's largest new and second hand bookshop. An Aladdin's cave for readers, it has an extensive stock in just about every subject, plus an extensive selection of academic texts for the local student crowd. It's more than just books that are treasured here – they host an award-winning events programme, vinyl store and Dillon's café. This historic bookshop is perfect for burrowing down with a good read, slice of cake and cuppa. Alternatively, the neighbouring Gordon and Tavistock Squares offer the tranquillity you need on fine days.
82a Gower Street, WC1E 6EQ;
waterstones.com

Eat & Drink

⑯ Andrew's Restaurant
Where journo's and cabbie's meet
The last of a dying breed, this working men's café is busy from 6am during the week, with local labourers chowing down on simple yet superb set breakfasts, served on original Formica tables. But they're not alone – media types from surrounding institutions love this family-run place for its classic British menu, service and décor. Expect no frills and cheap prices for your Shepherd's Pie or Scampi and Chips. Andrew's is as authentic as they come.
160 Grays Inn Road, WC1X 8ED; 020 7837 1630

⑰ Bloomsbury Farmers Market
Secret hot & fresh food haven
In one of the main squares of the University of London, overlooked by the Orwellian Senate House, is a weekly food market run by the London Farmers Markets organisation. It's a local, intimate affair, with regular stallholders and punters on their lunch breaks mingling over the produce and takeaway food on offer. There's a limited selection of fruit & veg, dairy and baked goods, with the stalls selling crab pastas, vegan paellas, and dosas taking centre stage.
Torrington Square, WC1E 7LE;
lfm.org.uk; open Thursday 09.00-14.00

⑱ Ciao Bella
La Dolce Vita on Lamb's Conduit
The photo-studded walls of Ciao Bella nod to countless memories made here. The cooking is reliably good and affordable – classic wines accompany traditional Italian dishes made with the love and skill you'd expect from a family business with 30 years' experience. Napoletana pizzas, spaghetti alle vongole and veal escalope – dishes that define our love affair with cooking absorbed from Continental holidays and mid-century migration. The service is efficient, if abrupt, and the pianist is a slice of La Dolce Vita that inspires this place.
86-90 Lamb's Conduit Street, WC1N 3LZ;
ciaobellarestaurant.co.uk

⑲ The Duke
Rare Art Deco delight
Once the Duke of York, the name might be the only thing that's changed at this historic 1930s pub. Housed in the Grade II listed Art Deco Mytre House is an exemplary interior of the inter-war style – rhubarb colour walls, leather booths and lots of linoleum. As for the food and drink, it's what your grandparents would recognise, with a few real ales on tap to accompany platefuls of sausage or pie and mash. While interesting & photogenic, this is a real pub and one perfect for a pint on your day out in Bloomsbury.
7 Roger Street, WC1N 2PB;
dukepub.co.uk

Bloomsbury - Eat & Drink

⑳ The Lamb
Cornerstone of the Conduit
The Lamb is a local institution. The pub has a remarkable history – Grade II listed; Dickens, Ted Hughes and Sylvia Plath have all enjoyed a drink here. It remains one of the few pubs with 'snob screens' to preserve well-to-do drinkers' privacy. The entire interior is a trip down memory lane, with racing green leather booths and wood-clad walls adorned with antique frames. Food and drink is standard fair but the atmosphere isn't to be missed, cranking up a notch when there's a rugby or quiz night.
94 Lamb's Conduit Street, WC1N 3LZ;
thelamblondon.com

㉑ Noble Rot
The magic behind the magazine
This restaurant is run by the people behind the namesake magazine – the authority on food & wine for a new generation. Tradition and innovation are well balanced in this tastefully converted Georgian townhouse, that features a Parisian-style wine bar and sprawling dining room. The award-winning wine list is as you'd expect from Noble Rot, while the food menu is concise and seasonal with dishes such as grilled Cornish John Dory, Burrata salad and chocolate & cherry Mille-Feuille. Catch the lunchtime set menu deal for an affordable foray into thoroughly fine dining.
51 Lamb's Conduit Street, WC1N 3NB;
noblerot.co.uk

㉒ Otto's
Haute Cuisine with a hint of humour
A favourite of food journalists and critics, Otto's is a hallmark of French fine dining. The waiters' suits are as stiffly ironed as the white tablecloths and steak tartare is fittingly served out of a silver dish, then smothered in foie gras, truffle or caviar. It's not cheap, but great food shouldn't be, and Otto's serves only to this standard, be it Bresse chicken on their a la carte or the lobster and duck set menus. The wine list is straight to the point, no-nonsense bottles from the finest French terroirs. While glamorous, there is a hint of a whimsical French irregularity to the design of the restaurant itself. If you feel haute cuisine is something one ought to experience before you die, then Otto's is one of few places outside of France to enjoy it.
182 Grays Inn Road, WC1X 8EW;
ottos-restaurant.com

Outdoors

㉓ Brunswick Square Gardens
Public square in the heart of Bloomsbury

This lush square was laid out in 1796 as part of the Foundling Hospital and named after Queen Caroline of Brunswick. It was built by James Burton who was also responsible for the grand Georgian housing that surrounded the square as well as much of Bloomsbury. The space was fashionable and featured in Jane Austin's *Emma*. The 20th century witnessed the demolition of all Burton's buildings but the square survived and is now Grade II listed. It's a great place to chill on warm days and is located just to the east of the Brunswick Centre.

Brunswick Square, WC1 1DN;

㉔ Coram's Fields
A unique child-friendly garden

London often feeling like an adult's playground, but this celebrated public garden is entirely dedicated to the interests of children. Adults may only enter when supervised by someone under-16. The garden is a tree-lined oasis, containing multiple sports courts, a pool, playground, café and farm. Wildlife projects, bands and circus acts are also a feature of the summer months. Look out for the many works of public art in the park, such as a pair of bronze mittens by Tracey Emin.

93 Guildford Street, WC1 1DN;
coramsfields.org

㉕ Gordon Square (w/ Momo's Garden Café)
A fine square with a great café

Originally a private residents' square, with surrounding houses once occupied by the Bloomsbury Set now marked out by blue plaques. Gordon Square is now owned by the University of London and open to the public, like it's symmetrical neighbour Tavistock Square. A highlight is the kiosk where Momo's Garden Café offers inexpensive vegetarian food with their own freshly baked cakes and other treats.

Gordon Square, WC1H 0PQ;
London.ac.uk

㉖ St George's Gardens
Tranquil park in a former cemetery

This three acre site was established as a burial ground for St George the Martyr and St George's Bloomsbury in 1713. The burial ground was full by 1850 and in the 1880s it was converted into the unusual park you find today. The more modest burial stones have been moved to the periphery of the park, but the larger monuments remain as striking park statuary. St George's is a little difficult to find, tucked away behind the better known Coram Fields and Brunswick Square, but is well worth seeking out for its tranquil atmosphere and remarkable history.

Heathcoate Street, WC1H 8HZ;
friendsofstgeorgesgardens.org.uk

Bloomsbury - Outdoors

㉗ Russell Square
Busy square in the heart of Bloomsbury

Developed by James Burton on behalf of the 5th Duke of Bedford and completed in 1804, this is Bloomsbury's largest and most popular square. Its popularity stems from it being behind the British Museum, with its own tube station and surrounded by some of London's most prestigious academic institutions. Among the notable features are a fountain, mature trees and planted beds, all presided over by an impressive monument to the Duke who founded the square over 200 years ago. There's a café in the park, but the Victorian cabmen's shelter on the north corner is a charming alternative.

Bloomsbury Square, WC1B 5EH

㉘ Tavistock Square
Green space dedicated to peace

This grand Georgian Square offers a welcome respite from the surrounding bustle of Bloomsbury. Many squares in London have military monuments, so Tavistock stands out with its monuments dedicated to peace and non-violence. Mahatma Gandhi's statue stands in the square's centre, and to the north is a commemorative stone for conscientious objectors. Nearby, the Hiroshima Tree remembers the victims of the first atomic bomb. The tree was planted in 1967 and grown from the seeds of one of the city's surviving cherry trees. Tavistock Square also has a bust of Virginia Woolf, close to her last home.

Tavistock Square, WC1H 9LG

Soho

London's Soho is the original Soho, and none of its imitators have quite caught up in prestige. A fashionable area from its inception, it has been a place for the wealthy to live and the capital's residents to be entertained for centuries. Soho was developed in the late 17th century following the Great Fire, as the aristocracy developed farmland west of the cramped streets of the medieval City. Over the centuries the aristocracy moved further west and Soho was settled by Italian and Jewish immigrants. In the 20th century it became famous for its nightlife and thriving sex industry. In the last 40 years gentrification has removed some rough edges and charm from the place but has also returned it to being one of the most desirable and expensive areas in the city, with multimillion pound properties and upmarket shops & restaurants. The most enduring legacy of its sexually liberal past is the presence of the gay community around Old Compton Street, while its reputation as the top entertainment district has been kept alive by the West End. Between Chinatown and Dean Street there are countless noteworthy places to eat, from inexpensive Italian caffs to centuries old French institutions. Despite the changes, Soho is still a magical place to enjoy a day out, but really comes alive when night falls. If you're planning in advance then a trip to one of the many acclaimed theatres is never amiss, but if visiting on a whim then The National Gallery is sure to satisfy. Afterward, wander in the direction of Chinatown and Soho Square for food, where you'll be utterly spoiled for choice. Finally, although there are so many spots to choose from, you won't find a more perfect place to end an evening than at the legendary Ronnie Scott's – a jazz bar that, like many of the nearby pubs and eateries, is keeping the spirit of 'old Soho' alive.

SOHO

1. Chinatown
2. The National Gallery
3. Photographers' Gallery
4. Prince Charles Cinema
5. Ronnie Scott's
6. The West End
7. Berwick Street
8. Carnaby Street
9. Denmark Street
10. Foyles Bookshop
11. Liberty
12. Bar Bruno
13. Bar Italia
14. The French House
15. Maison Bertaux
16. Pierre Victoire
17. Quo Vadis
18. Phoenix Garden
19. Soho Square

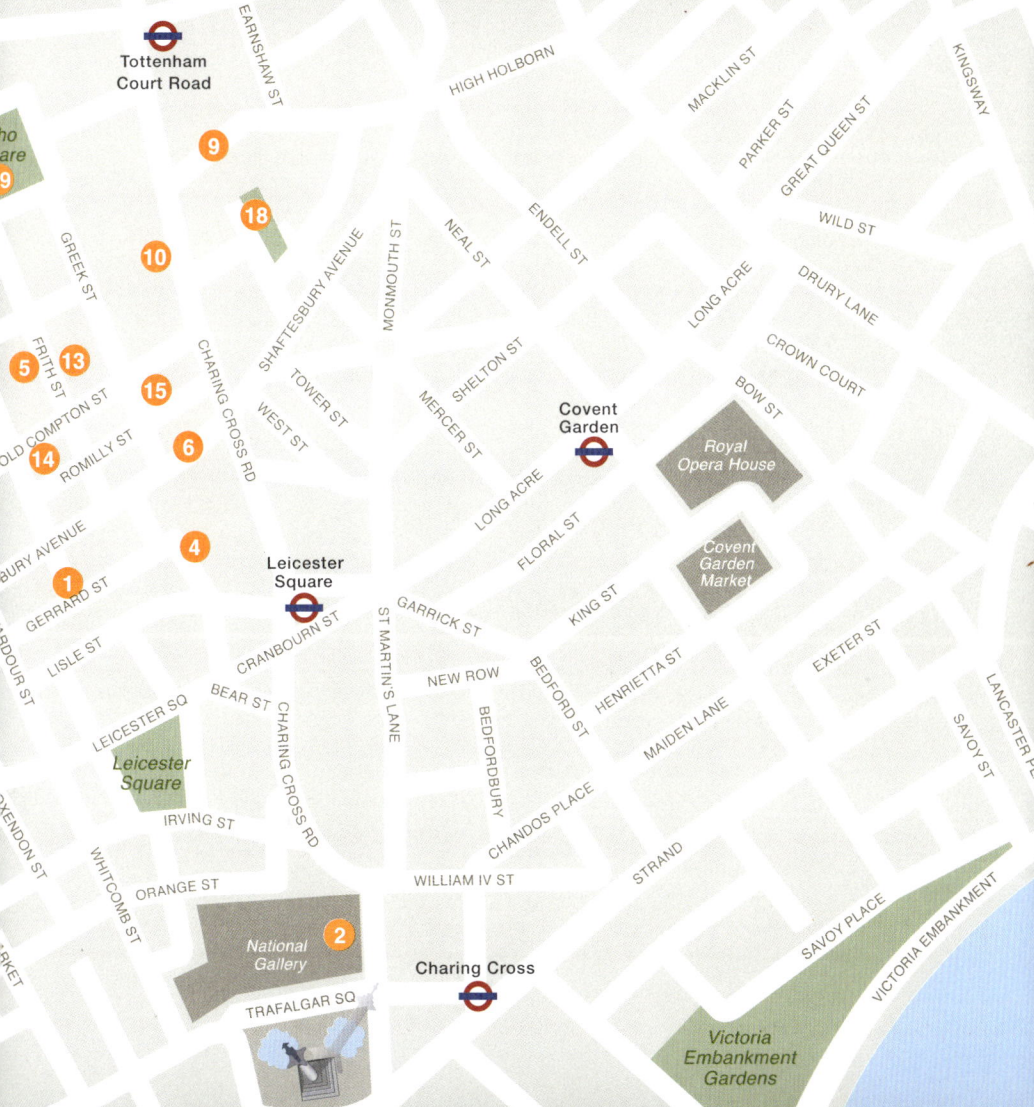

Visit

❶ Chinatown
Shanghai in Soho

Recent redevelopment has eroded some of Soho's character, but Chinatown is as vibrant as ever and remains the best place to experience a much-loved cuisine, as well as the New Year's celebrations that take place here. With the ornate gate on Wardour Street, scores of restaurants, specialty grocers and acupuncturists lining Gerrard Street, and red lanterns as far as the eye can see, it's easy to feel immersed in something out of your ordinary. Dim Sum and Siu Mei are two unmissable features of the culinary landscape. For the latter, there are a wealth of notable options. Many consider the Peking duck at Four Seasons the best in the city, at least at affordable prices, although the massive, multi-story Wong Kei and tiny Café TPT both give it a run for its money with their char siu pork. Meanwhile, Kowloon Bakery is a solid option for picking up a steamed bun, while Beijing Dumpling and Dumplings' Legend are especially good at, well, it isn't hard to guess. Old Town 97 is one of the few places still open at 3am for late-night revellers to soak up their sins, and Good Friend Chicken's fried goods and bubble tea are a hit with the younger crowds that still favour exploring Chinatown during the daytime.
Gerrard Street, W1D 5QA;
chinatown.co.uk

❷ The National Gallery
A mecca for Fine Art

Amid the pigeons, protestors and punters of Trafalgar Square are crowds of art lovers visiting the National Gallery. The gallery offers a permanent collection of over 2,300 paintings that span 700 years of Western European art history. Here you can enjoy some of the world's most famous paintings, including Van Gogh's *Sunflowers*, Van Eyck's *The Arnolfini Portrait*, and Leonardo da Vinci's *Virgin of the Rocks*. The paintings are arranged chronologically, beginning in the Sainsbury Wing, before the West Wing's High Renaissance and Mannerist paintings, then the North Wing's Baroque art, which includes Vermeer's *Young Woman Standing at a Virginal* and the gallery's collection of Rembrandts. Finally, the East Wing covers Impressionism during the 19th and early 20th centuries, with works by Monet and Renoir. Visitors can explore the collection via a variety of guides, including free live tours. Temporary exhibitions, films, courses, and lectures are also frequent. For those seeking respite, the gallery has lots of comfortable seating, and three in-house dining options, from a mural-lined dining room serving a seasonal menu, to brasserie-style waiter service and self-service options. The gallery's shops sell art related gifts, with a print-on-demand service available for reproductions. Best of all, entry is free of charge for the permanent collection.
Trafalgar Square, WC2N 5DN; 020 7747 2885;
nationalgallery.org.uk

Soho - Visit

❸ Photographers' Gallery
London's first photography gallery

Established in 1971, the Photographers' Gallery was the UK's first independent gallery dedicated to photography. It showcases fine art and photojournalism through an exhibition program that promotes new talents alongside established names. It also hosts the *Deutsche Börse Photography Foundation Prize*, recognising the best European photographers. In addition to exhibitions, they offer lectures and workshops with artists. The gallery's gift shop is renowned for its collection of photography books, and the Print Sales Gallery sells vintage, modern, and contemporary prints. Visitors can even purchase cameras and film before relaxing in the cosy café.

16-18 Ramillies Street, W1F 7LW;
thephotographersgallery.org.uk

❹ Prince Charles Cinema
The crown jewel for cinephiles

Many of Soho's marvels were established in the Swinging Sixties, and the Prince Charles Cinema was part of that transformation. It started life as a theatre and then quickly morphed into showing pornographic films at a time when this part of town was infamous for sex trade. Nowadays the Prince Charles is perhaps London's best-known repertory cinema, dedicated to reviving classic and cult films, regularly rotated alongside a roster of contemporary arthouse and box-office movies. Screenings of rarely shown works by auteurs in 35mm, 70mm and even VHS add to the magic, while sing-alongs, genre-and-director seasons, movie marathon nights and Q&A sessions with directors and actors ensure there's always something interesting happening at the Prince Charles. The theatre itself also has a distinctive satellite dish curve to the floor of the stalls, meaning that audiences are sat at an upwards angle as they face the stage, made all the cosier by velvet seats in the bottom rows and leather ones at the top. The Prince Charles is a remnant of a bygone era and, alas, the last independent cinema in the West End, so ensure you stop by to support this unique institution.

7 Leicester Place, WC2H 7BY; 020 7494 3654;
princecharlescinema.com

❺ Ronnie Scott's
UK's undisputed king of jazz clubs

Ronnie Scott's is simply a must-visit destination for jazz lovers, music enthusiasts and anyone in need of a show-stopping late-night date spot. Established by the eponymous owner in 1959, the club has become a legendary venue globally for hosting some of the world's most prominent musicians, in jazz and other genres – it was even the site of Jimi Hendrix's last public performance. Before you enter, you'll see some of the most recognisable neon lighting left in what was once the most illuminated part of town. The club's interior meanwhile stays dimly lit by the individual table lamps that sit atop velour booths, creating a cosy, classy ambience. The acoustics are the best around, and it helps that you're just feet away from the performers. Programming covers traditional and contemporary styles, with jam sessions featuring underground artists alongside established names. And with the swanky upstairs space staying open till 3am, Ronnie Scott's remains one of the last spots to still offer an early hour's experience. What's more, you'll struggle to find a better cocktail at any of the many bars found on Frith Street, while the food on offer fits perfectly with the unaffected sophistication of the environment.

47 Frith St, W1D 4HT;
ronniescotts.co.uk

❻ The West End
Theatreland – Britain's answer to Broadway

Along with NYC's Broadway, shows in the West End are generally regarded as the best commercial theatre in the English-speaking world. Seeing one is a bucket-list activity for many tourists in London – over 16 million attended in 2022. Famous screen actors, British and international alike, frequently perform at the 39 theatres. They are following a tradition that began in 1663 with the opening of the Theatre Royal, Drury Lane. Likewise, many well-known plays, from *Alice in Wonderland* to *Pygmalion*, won their acclaim here. Roughly bordered by Oxford Street to the north, Kingsway to the east, the Strand to the south and Regent Street to the west, with prominent streets like Shaftesbury Avenue in between, a trip to Theatreland offers more than musicals, plays, and big-ticket comedy nights. Many of the buildings are late-Victorian or Edwardian and have protected status, ensuring they remain architecturally impressive with preserved neo-classical, Romanesque, or Victorian façades and luxurious, detailed interior design and decoration. However, it's not all about the past. The most successful shows, by the likes of Andrew Lloyd Webber and Elton John, have a more modern bent – think box-office hits such as *Hamilton* and *Les Mis* rather than Shakespeare or Wilde. But if you enjoy a sing-along, there's nowhere better for a day out in town.

westend.com

Shop

❼ Berwick Street
An Oasis, and the band's album cover
Berwick Street is the quintessential thoroughfare in Soho. The area flourished at the turn of the 18th century with pubs like The Green Man and Blue Posts and the historic market that is still running today. Alongside the few surviving fruit & veg stalls, you'll find Michelin-star restaurants and trendy cafés. But better still it threads together indie stores like Gosh! Comics with streetwear brands like Supreme, which once reliably saw queues of teenagers camping outside overnight for a chance at bagging their most prized releases. And in and around it you'll find London's highest concentration of record stores: Reckless Records, Sounds of the Universe, Phonica, Sister Ray and Rough Trade have all weathered the storm of digital streaming to find a place on the street. It's little wonder this street has been immortalised in art and advertising, with *(What's the Story) Morning Glory?* the most famous example.
Berwick St, W1F 8ST

❽ Carnaby Street
For the 'dedicated follower of fashion'
Dating to the 17th century, Carnaby Street is still Soho's most visited pedestrianised shopping street, famous as the epicentre of Swinging London in the Sixties. Although no longer as cutting-edge, you'll still find on-trend brands alongside a handful of indie enterprises in the surrounding streets. Moreover, once you've tired of shopping, you can access Kingly Court, a three-storied dining venue with an al fresco courtyard, bars and restaurants galore.
Carnaby Street, W1F 7DW

❾ Denmark Street
Tin Pan Alley off Tottenham Court Road
Since the 1950s Denmark Street has played a central part in British popular music, first as home to music publishers and later a place for recording studios and instrument shops – a blue plaque now commemorates this history. Its star-studded visitors include The Rolling Stones who recorded here and David Bowie who frequented the Gioconda café. Even Elton John and the Sex Pistols crossed paths as the pop star composed songs near the rock band's first flat. Shops from this period like Chris Bryant's Musical Instruments and Denmark Street Guitars still operate, the latter stocking over 3,000 instruments, including the UK's largest guitar selection. Specialist stores like Regent Sounds, Macaris, Argents and Rose, Morris & Co. are all still trading on this legendary street.
Denmark Street, WC2H 8LP

Soho - Shop

Soho - Shop

⑩ Foyles Bookshop
London's legendary bookseller
Foyles has been on Charing Cross Road for over a century, although in 2014 it moved to what was once Central Saint Martin's art college. The new building extends over 5 floors and remains part of a book selling tradition that goes back to the early 20th century when William and Gilbert Foyle founded the company. Now part of Waterstones, Foyles has kept some of its unique character. The shop holds regular literary events and also has a great café where you can relax and enjoy your latest literary purchase.

⑪ Liberty
London's most unique department store
Liberty is distinct amongst Westminster's several well-known department stores for how it works with emerging designers. The store also remains popular with designers looking for inspiration and trying to source unique materials for their own work. The store has collaborated with household names like William Morris, Yves Saint Laurent, and Vivienne Westwood. Liberty also helped popularize the Modern Style and Asian objets d'art. The Tudor revival exterior is made from two old HMS gunboats, a further example of just how unique Liberty's remains.
Great Marlborough Street, W1B 5AH;
libertylondon.com

Soho - Shop

Eat & Drink

⑫ Bar Bruno
A caff, not a café!

Although Soho was once full of them, its last surviving Italian caff is proof there's life in the old dog yet. Bar Bruno's shop front has changed, but the same Chesterfield booths draw in an eclectic crowd. Cabbies at 4am for eggs, bacon, chips and beans; the office lunch-dash for a sandwich; and the occasional supermodel for an unpretentious toast and tea. A Full English is as warranted as red sauce spaghetti, whilst if taking away, arancini is a great choice. Best of all, this family-run spot has stayed affordable when prices have risen so much in the area.
101 Wardour St, W1F 0UG

⑬ Bar Italia
Last of London's late-night life

London's waning nightlife has been lamented by many, with punitive licensing rules starving Soho of its character. Raise a glass at Bar Italia then, because this spot is open 21 hours a day, 7 days a week, ensuring revellers can get a negroni, espresso or arancini after spilling out from the surrounding pubs and bars at almost any hour. Open since 1949 and still run by the same family, with one of the most recognisable neon signs and charmingly old-school interiors around, there's little wonder it's a favourite for locals and those wanting a taste of traditional Soho.
22 Frith St, W1D 4RF;
baritaliasoho.co.uk

⑭ The French House
Where old Soho lives on

The history of the French House's barely fits on a page. This British institution was opened as the 'York Minster' by a German in 1891, sold to a Belgian at the outbreak of WWI, and run by his son from then until 1989. During the war de Gaulle was famously a regular customer, and would write many of his legendary speeches here. Later, it became a hangout for the likes of Dylan Thomas, Francis Bacon and Lucian Freud. It was always called 'the French House' in reference to the owners origins, but after a fire in 1984 this became the pub's official name. The pub is indeed very 'French' with more Ricard being sold here than anywhere else in Britain and you can only order beer by the half. Grade-II listed, with a no phones policy in the intimate dining room. The French House retains all the charm of its bohemian past, but with an updated menu featuring the likes of rillettes, terrine and pommes aligot, best enjoyed with a bottle of their Bordeaux.
49 Dean St, W1D 5BG;
frenchhousesoho.com

⓯ Maison Bertaux
London's oldest pâtisserie

Tearooms were once commonplace in Britain, but London's oldest pâtisserie is one of the last left. There are over 20 varieties of tea on offer to be enjoyed with the cakes and fancies made on the premises daily. They opened in 1871 and can boast both Karl Marx and Virginia Woolf as former patrons. Marzipan figs and Mont Blancs are favourites, although you can't go wrong with tarte tatin or eclairs. Keep an eye out for the charming blue shop front, which welcomes you into the homely space presided over by the indomitable Wade sisters. A warm macaroon from Maison Bertaux is one of life's great pleasures, if you're luck you can even choose yours straight from the tray.

28 Greek St, W1D 5DQ; maisonbertaux.com

⓰ Pierre Victoire
Inexpensive bistro near the West End

For a quick pre-or-post-matinee meal, this charmingly old-school French bistro is more than enough. At roughly £20 for the two course set menu, you can enjoy culinary classics like steak frites, french onion soup, beef bourguignon and confit duck without breaking the bank, which is welcome considering the sky-high prices of theatre tickets these days. Just a stone's throw from Tottenham Court Road station, and open from midday till late every day of the week, Pierre Victoire has few frills, but is decorated with the vintage film posters and wooden furniture you'd imagine in a restaurant of the République.

5 Dean Street, W1D 3RQ; pierrevictoire.com

⓱ Quo Vadis
If not here, then where are you going?

If one restaurant could encapsulate London, it would be Quo Vadis. An almost 100-year-old Latin-named Italian restaurant that gave French names to their dishes when Italian cuisine was less well known and admired. The restaurant was once co-owned by Marco Pierre White and Damien Hirst. The building is now Grade-I listed because of its association with Karl Marx, who lived upstairs in the 1850s. Today it serves an indomitable British menu thanks to chef Jeremy Lee and owners Sam and Eddie Hart (who also run Barrafina, the Michelin-starred tapas joint next-door). The smoked eel sandwich is unmissable, as are the pies that feature regularly rotating fillings, and puddings, which tip their hat to classics like Île flotant. The neon signage outside is as recognisable as the regally avant-garde interior, making a meal here something to remember.

26-29 Dean Street, W1D 3LL;
quovadissoho.co.uk

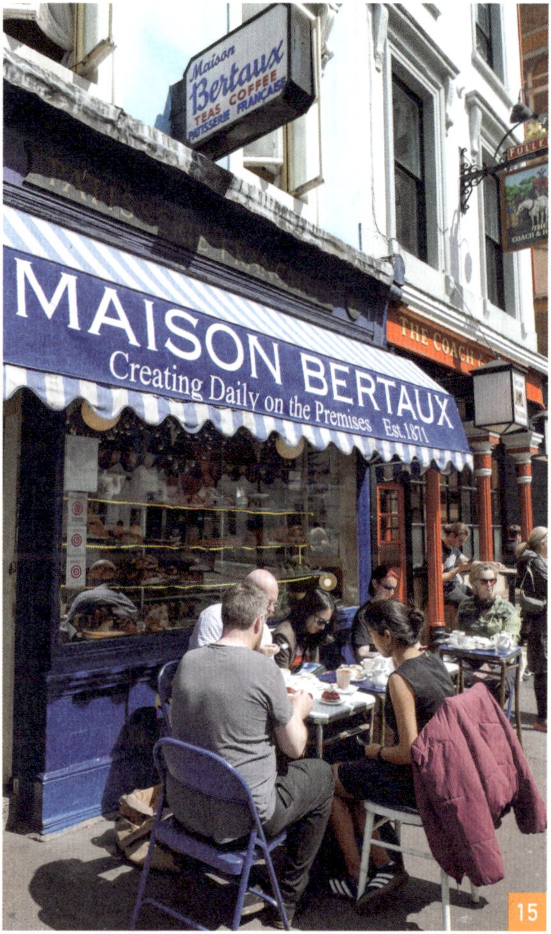
Maison
Bertaux
TEAS COFFEE
PATISSERIE FRANÇAISE
MAISON BERTAUX
Creating Daily on the Premises Est.1871
15

17

17

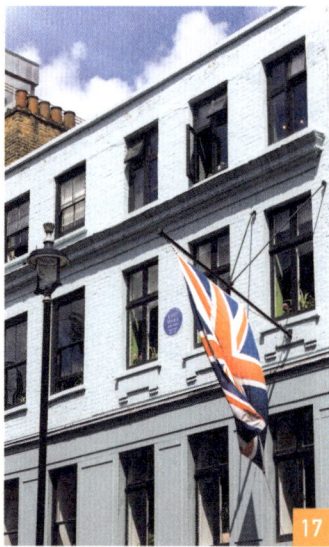

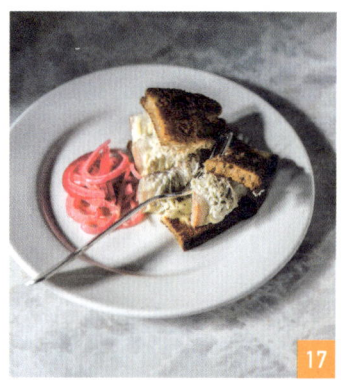

Outdoors

⑱ Phoenix Garden
Covent Garden's Community Garden

This community garden was established on a car park behind the Phoenix Theatre on Charing Cross Road in 1984. Historically, the area was largely residential, although now it's the last vestige of green space amongst the vast offices and shops with the iconic Centre Point looming in the distance. Phoenix Garden has survived various challenges, including a major industrial fly-tipping incident soon after its foundation. It is now the only surviving of the original seven Covent Garden community gardens. Apart from providing respite from the surrounding busy streets, it hosts regular social events, including an annual agricultural show and volunteering workshops. Having escaped closure in 2016, Phoenix Gardens remains a rare oasis of calm in the West End and a perfect place to relax and catch your breath on a day out in Soho.

21 Stacey St, WC2H 8DG; thephoenixgarden.org

⑲ Soho Square
A park fit for a king

Soho Square has been a public park since 1954, but its origins date back to the late 1600s. A much-weathered statue of Charles II has stood there (with an extended interruption) since shortly after the restoration of the monarchy. Many of the surrounding buildings are listed, with numbers 10 and 15 dating from the square's opening. The offices are now occupied by blue-chip media organisations and the square was once home to the head quarters of The Beatles' Apple Records. Meanwhile, Saint Patrick's Catholic Church, the French Protestant Church of London and the House of St Barnabas provide fundraising and outreach for destitute locals, a spirit of charity championed by the square's most famous resident – Mary Seacole. A mock Tudor building stands in the centre, whilst underneath remain catacombs and a WWII air-raid shelter. The Square has been a popular reference point in literature, including in *A Tale of Two Cities* and *My Fair Lady*. The singer-song writer Kirsty MacColl (1959-2000) wrote the lyrics 'One day I'll be Waiting There, No Empty Bench on Soho Square' and this is inscribed on a memorial bench in her memory. Today, the square is still very busy and there are few empty benches when the weather is fare.

Soho Square, W1D 3QP

Barbican

Barbican is among the most recognisable and visited parts of London, but it hasn't been that way for long. The name derives from the Latin word for a fortified gate, and Roman ruins are still visible in the area once known as Cripplegate. It was almost entirely destroyed during the Blitz, leaving less than 50 residents by the 1950s. The Brutalist Barbican Estate we now know and love was built between 1965 and 1976 by Chamberlin, Powell and Bon. Unlike their first project on nearby Golden Lane, Barbican was marketed to the affluent and is now among the most sought-after neighbourhoods in London. Its location in the historic heart of London, alongside ancient churches and markets has created a unique architecture and ambience. To enjoy a day out here, walk around and soak it all in. Start at the Barbican Centre. Even if you don't see one of the incredible exhibitions, plays, operas or other events they have on, you'll enjoy this marvel by circumnavigating it. Mind you, museums aren't exactly in short supply: both the Charterhouse and Order of St John reveal how much history lies in these streets, as does making a pit stop at Postman's Park. Nearby are several long-established Italian caffs with their original decor mostly intact, serving some of the best Full English breakfasts and sandwiches in town. They also tell the story of how Italian immigration has influenced the area. However, if you were to make a reservation at any restaurant in London, make it the iconic St JOHN.

BARBICAN

1. The Barbican Centre
2. The Charterhouse
3. Four Corner Chess Club
4. Museum of the Order of St John
5. Smithfield Market
6. St Bartholomew the Great
7. Embassy Electrical Supplies
8. International Magic Shop
9. magCulture (*off map*)
10. Sway Gallery Japanese Store
11. Beppe's Café
12. Giddy Up Coffee
13. L. Terroni & Sons
14. Scotti's Snack Bar
15. St JOHN
16. Whitecross Street Market
17. Ye Olde Mitre
18. Barbican Conservatory
19. Fortune Street Park
20. Postman's Park

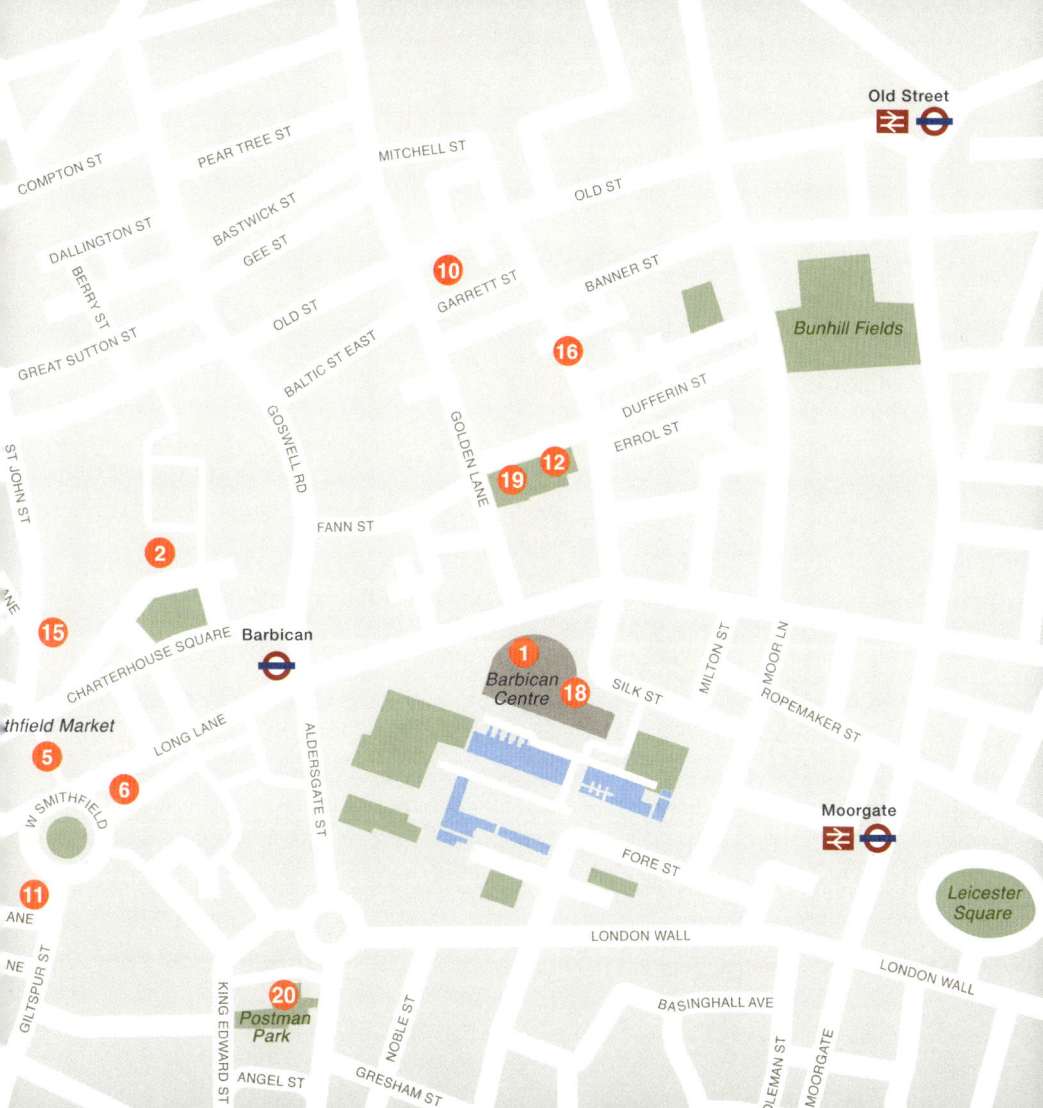

Visit

❶ The Barbican Centre
Largest performing arts centre in Europe

Although Brutalism is as divisive as Marmite, the consensus today is that the Barbican Centre is one of the greatest of the movement's achievements. It hasn't always been so, with the ziggurat being voted London's ugliest building around the same time it was given Grade II* listed status, just 20 years after its opening. Built side-by-side with the most historic parts of the city, in an area badly bombed during WWII and now associated with the finance industry, it was intended by its architects Chamberlin, Powell and Bon, along with the surrounding estate, to provide a utopia of sorts. And a utopia of sorts it is, for today you can experience some of the best art on offer in London, both at The Curve and main gallery, or else walk around magnificent ponds and gardens, take the edge off at the bars and restaurants, or catch a show at any one of the three cinema screens, two theatres or concert hall. When the weather permits, there are few better ways to spend a day than at the Lakeside Terrace, where you'll find plenty of other people relaxing, whether with a beer, a game of ping pong or simply soaking in the view. If you've got little ones to think about, then check out the regular free events run at the children's library.

Silk St, EC2Y 8DS; barbican.org.uk

❷ The Charterhouse
A monastery turned museum

Originally a Carthusian monastery, this building has been many things since its completion in 1371, including a cemetery for victims of the Black Death, a private Tudor mansion and its current function as a charity. This latter purpose was established by Thomas Sutton in 1611, who wanted to provide education for the young and an almshouse for the old. As well as the charitable work there is also a museum charting its 650-year history. Although many of the objects on display are stunning, including the collection of 17th-century Flemish tapestries, nothing quite compares to the Grand Chamber, which Elizabeth I used for meeting with her Privy Council. A twice daily tours of the grounds are the best way to soak all this history in. The tours cover different themes and are occasionally done by candlelight.

Charterhouse Square, EC1M 6AN; thecharterhouse.org; Open: Tues-Sat

❸ Four Corner Chess Club

If you're exploring this neighbourhood on a Saturday afternoon, don't miss the Four Corner chess club that meets up between 12 and 3.30 on St John's Square to enjoy some open air chess. The club is open to all from budding Grand Masters to total beginners and is always well attended. It's a unique aspect of this unique part of town.

St John's Square, EC1V 4JJ; fourcornerclub (Insta)

4 Museum of the Order of St John
Holiest of history museums

A Tudor gatehouse, one-time entrance to the medieval priory of the Order of St John, is the picturesque setting for this museum. It tells the 1000-year story of the order, from its foundation during the Crusades to its modern endeavours as the St John Ambulance. Warlike defender of the faith on one hand, merciful provider for the poor and sick on the other, the original Order has a complicated history. The displays in the gallery follow the changing fortunes of these warrior monks over the centuries, as they migrated around various Mediterranean strongholds. Exhibits include rare armour, ancient coins, portraits of eminent Hospitallers and a gallery dedicated to the history of their ambulance service. You can also visit the Cloister Garden, planted with medicinal herbs to recall the Order's caring vocation. Guided tours take about an hour and give access to parts of the gatehouse otherwise closed to the public, such as the magnificent wood-panelled Chapter Hall, the Church and Crypt. The 12th-century crypt is a rare example of Norman architecture in London and the location of a memento mori effigy of the last Prior, William Weston. He is said to have died of a broken heart after Henry VIII's dissolution of the Order of St John in 1540.

St John's Gate, 26 St John's Lane, EC1M 4DA
museumstjohn.org.uk

⑤ Smithfield Market
A cathedral of carnivory
Meat has been sold at Smithfield Market for over eight hundred years. The present building dates from 1866, but beneath the iron girders you'll find modern market counters, making it a more pleasant place to shop for the public. Although at its busiest in the early hours of the morning, trade does continue until lunchtime. All this is destined to change with plans to move the operation to Dagenham in the coming years, so visit before this historic institution disappears.
Charterhouse Street, EC1A 9PS

⑥ St Bartholomew the Great
The 'hidden church'
One of London's finest Norman churches, the Great was the centre of an Augustinian priory founded in 1123 by Prior Rahere. After the dissolution of the priory in 1539, the core of the building became the parish church, while various other parts were used over the years as, among other things, private dwellings, a print works, stable, non-conformist meeting place and various schools. The Great underwent a major Victorian restoration led by the architect Sir Aston Webb. Rahere's remains are in the tomb built to the left of the High Altar, overlooked from the right by the rare oriel window dating from about 1517. Other highlights include the Cloister and a striking Damien Hirst sculpture. The church has featured in numerous films, including *Four Weddings and a Funeral* and *Shakespeare in Love*.
West Smithfield, EC1A 9DS; greatstbarts.com

Barbican - Shop

Shop

❼ Embassy Electrical Supplies
One of London's most unusual shops

For more than 20 years Mehmet Murat has sold from his electrical supply shop what is now widely considered some of the best olive oil available in the UK. The oil is hand-bottling and pressed from his family's olive groves in Cyprus. Although strange to some, Mr Olive Oil – as he is known by many – is simply carrying on a practice that was commonplace in his home village of selling your farm surplus. Alongside the olive oil, he also stocks preserved lemons, pomegranate molasses, sweet paprika, candied walnuts, chilli flakes, and of course wires, light bulbs and fuses.

76 Compton St, EC1V 0BN; mroliveoil.com

❽ International Magic Shop
London's last magic shop

Having been in the business of trickery since 1958, the family-run shop International Magic is unlike anything else in London, literally. It is the only magic shop left in town, the others having disappeared (and not in a puff of smoke). From coin tricks to card decks, as well as books and DVDs, you can get anything an aspiring or professional magician could want. Owner Martin is on hand to advise on all magical matters, including events at places like the nearby Magic Circle – that is, unless he pulls a Houdini.

89 Clerkenwell Road, EC1R 5BX; internationalmagic.com

❾ magCulture
Print lover's paradise

magCulture began life as... a magazine, and soon after morphed into a blog, before becoming a bricks-and-mortar business in 2015. So if you want to pick up some independent publishing, this is the place. The white-cube of a space, furnished by Vitsoe, displays 700+ titles from around the world. Visitors are encouraged to browse, with knowledgeable staff on standby to advise. Plus, the stock can be shipped locally and globally. Do check their website for info on the regular events they host.

270 St John Street, EC1V 4PE; magculture.com

❿ Sway Gallery Japanese Store
Go-to gift shop for Japanophiles

Since 2016 Sway Gallery has been the go-to destination for Japanese art and goods in London. Half gallery, half concept store, you can catch an exhibition before perusing the handmade home décor and artisanal kitchenware on offer. Much of what's on show is from up-and-coming artists and makers from Japan. Other items, like their selection of Japanese tools and utensils, are from heritage producers with an international reputation for excellence in craftsmanship, forged over sometimes hundreds of years of practice. Despite this, prices are quite reasonable, so make sure to check them out when meandering through Barbican's back streets.

70-72 Old Street, EC1V 9AN; london.sway-gallery.com

Eat & Drink

⑪ Beppe's Café
90-year-old caff next to the market
The old-school signage is the first thing you notice about this much-loved family-run caff, before you step through the green-tiled doorway into a wood-clad interior that hasn't changed in decades. Beppe's – an abbreviation of Giuseppe, the name of its founder – is a reminder of how there are more Italians in London than anywhere outside Italy, many of whom were vital in shaping our culture of eating out. Here, the meat comes straight from the market, so the fry-ups are top quality while still affordable.
23 West Smithfield, EC1A 9HY

⑫ Giddy Up Coffee in Fortune Street Park
A pick-me-up en plein air
When it comes to grabbing a coffee to go, you'd be hard-pressed to find better than Giddy Up. Trading from a converted tool shed in the low-key but lovely Fortune Street Park, you can satisfy your caffeine needs with views of the Barbican. The family that runs the business are experts when it comes to beans and preparation, plus they sell a great assortment of homemade sweet treats. What's more, there are regular events put on by the people that call this part of town home, plus a great playground for those with kids to keep entertained.
Fortune Street Park, 18 Fortune Street, EC1Y 0SB

⑬ L. Terroni & Sons
London's oldest Italian deli
Running since 1878, the pedigree at Terroni's is what you'd expect from almost 150 years in business. Cured goods and other Italian products line the walls, much of which is used to make pastas and sandwiches you can enjoy eating in. But if you're in a hurry, this historic establishment is just as good for espresso and pastries like sfogliatelle, made fresh every morning. Terroni's is a unique place and one well worth making a special effort to visit.
138 Clerkenwell Road, EC1R 5DL, terroni.co.uk

⑭ Scotti's Snack Bar
The lifeblood of London's Little Italy
It'd be somewhat remiss to call Scotti's a caff since they don't serve fried breakfasts. It's more a living museum of post-war Britain when supper was as simple as a sandwich and cuppa. Formica surfaces and friendly Italo-Londoner staff are another throwback to its opening in 1967 when this part of town was a stopping point for newly arrived migrants. The place has survived because of the great sandwiches, particularly the chicken escalope, and the loyal clientele of locals and cabbies.
38 Clerkenwell Green, EC1R 0DU

⑮ St JOHN
Patron saint of British cooking

Food and restaurants would never be the same after Fergus Henderson and Trevor Gulliver opened their restaurant in 1994. Cult status came almost immediately, and a Michelin star followed in 2009. Today, many still think it's the best restaurant in London, and its impact has been global. Anthony Bourdain called it 'the restaurant of his dreams' and Henderson 'a walking Buddha for chefs'. Why? Arguably it is the nose-to-tail cooking pioneered here. Every menu that features seasonal, local or overlooked ingredients owes a debt to the cooking at St JOHN. Once commonplace things like their signature bone marrow had all but disappeared from British plates until then. None of this is jingoistic. Much about St JOHN is modern and European, not least the French wine list, and meat-free dishes are reliably excellent. Pudding, meanwhile, is a highlight rather than an afterthought. Madeleines are a must-order, and all the food has that quality of 'just like mother used to make'. Named after the street they're on, the familiarity with offal and Spartan interior make sense considering Smithfield is next door and the premises was previously a bacon smokery and Communist Party HQ. Presentation is unaffected and the prices are reasonable. Many notable chefs are disciples, while their cookbooks have biblical significance for home cooks. Most customers are loyal followers, but even for the as-yet-unconverted, a trip to this temple of British cuisine will inspire devotion.

26 St John St, EC1M 4AY; stjohnrestaurant.com

⑯ Whitecross Street Market
A new kind of market in an old part of town

What was once a struggling traditional weekday market full of fruit & veg stalls has transformed in recent years into a street food market, where local workers come to peruse the vast selection of cuisines on offer. From Buddha bowls and katsu curry to Turkish kebabs and Swedish meatballs with mash, you can get just about anything. Vegans and vegetarians are well-catered for by spots like Village Kitchen, as are sweet tooths by the many stalls offering baked goods. Meanwhile, for those fancying a tipple, The Two Brewers pub allows you to take in food if you order a pint. Alternatively, there are plenty of parks and open spaces nearby, like Fortune Street Park and the Barbican Centre, where you can sit down and enjoy a lunchtime break.

Whitecross Street, EC1Y 8QP;
whitecross-street-market.co.uk

⑰ Ye Olde Mitre
Holiest of public houses

This Grade II listed public house is one of London's most recognisable pubs. Built in 1546 for the inconspicuous servants of the Bishops of Ely, it's famous for having a cherry tree that Queen Elizabeth once danced around. The pub was nominally a part of Cambridge and the licensees used to have to travel there to renew their licence. Featured on the Campaign for Real Ale's National Inventory of Historic Pub Interiors and run by Fullers, you're sure to enjoy a pint here.

1 Ely Court, EC1N 6SJ; yeoldemitreholborn.co.uk

Outdoors

⑱ Barbican Conservatory
Second largest conservatory in London
The Barbican Conservatory is a little-known gem, despite being the second largest of its kind in London, after Kew. An idiosyncratic afterthought, it was built around the fly tower of the Arts Centre theatre and opened in 1984, with a cacti-filled Arid House being added two years later. The Conservatory is open on selected days and admission is free, with tickets for the following week released online every Friday at 10am – a limited number are available on the day. Here you can admire over 2,000 species of tropical and sub-tropical plants, plus the resident terrapins.
Silk Street, EC2Y 8DS; barbican.org.uk

⑲ Fortune Street Park
Pocket park in the city
The City is hardly known for its greenery, so it's places like Fortune Street Park that break the mould and provide respite amidst the concrete and steel. Sandwiched between the Barbican and Whitecross Street, the park was developed in a heavily bombed area, but in Elizabethan times was the site of a theatre. Today, it has a kid's playground, a great coffee shop (see p.56), and several benches where you can take something to eat or simply enjoy the peace and quiet. Several community events also run throughout the year.
18 Fortune Street, EC1Y 0SB;
fortunestreetpark.com

⑳ Postman's Park
Public garden with Grade-II* listed memorial
This historic city garden is well worth a visit. The former churchyard became a public park in 1880 and was popular with local postal workers. The park is now best known for the memorial wall – the inspiration of Victorian painter and philanthropist G.W. Watts – that records the heart-rending acts of bravery that led to the rescuer's death. Despite being shaded by surrounding buildings, an eclectic collection of plants thrives here, including the City's only publicly accessible horse chestnut tree.
King Edward Street, EC1A 7BT

North

Hampstead
Stoke Newington
Islington

Hampstead

Hampstead has been a 'homestead' since Saxon times, but despite all its natural qualities, few could have imagined its contemporary character. Now home to more millionaires than anywhere else in the country, and with many of the grand mansions now owned by billionaires, the area is synonymous with the elite and intelligentsia. Listing famous residents reads like a Who's Who, and you can spot 60 or so blue plaques across the neighbourhood. The rich flocked to live here for the incredible architecture and the tranquility of the Heath – London's largest ancient parkland. Development took off in the 17th century because of the presence of iron-rich water, sought out for its medicinal properties. Beautiful homes, many of them stately (and later some of them Modernist icons), were built here by those enthralled by the landscape. So, when visiting the Heath, you'll be in good company. A day out here is best spent wandering through the meadows and woodland, popping into the ponds on warmer days, and taking in the so-good-they're-legally-protected views of London's skyline from Parliament Hill. When you've had your fix, head to one of several amazing homes that surround it, like 2 Willow Road or Burgh House. Inside, you'll find insight into the history of the area, as well as acclaimed art and events. Finally, a stop at one of the many nearby pubs, each with its own story to tell, is in order.

Visit

❶ 2 Willow Road
A fine example of Modernism
A Modernist vision of a terraced house, 2 Willow Road is unlike any other National Trust property. Built by Ernö Goldfinger in 1937 and lived in until 1994, today it is one of only two Modernist homes in the UK open to the public. The interior includes furniture and toys designed by Goldfinger and work by Henry Moore, Bridget Riley, Max Ernst and Marcel Duchamp. A regular introductory video gives the history of this modernist masterpiece, whilst the rooftop terrace provides stunning views. Don't forget to pre-book this one-of-a-kind attraction.

2 Willow Road, NW3 1TH; nationaltrust.org.uk

❷ Burgh House
Historic house, gallery and arts centre
This Grade I listed Queen Anne house dates from 1704 and is located just off Hampstead's busy high street. It served as a private residence for much of its history but fell into disrepair until rescued by group of locals in 1979 and transformed into this local museum, arts centre and exhibition space. Don't miss the original staircase with fluted columns and barley-twist balusters which is one of the best features of the house. If all this art and architecture makes you hungry, there's a great café in the basement.

New End Square, NW3 1LT; burghhouse.org.uk

❸ Isokon Gallery
First Modernist block of flats in Britain
In the former garage of the Grade I listed Isokon building, this exhibition space is dedicated to all things Modernist. The block of flats was the first of its kind in Britain and pioneered minimalist city living. Walter Gropius, Marcel Breuer and Agatha Christie have all called one of these $25m^2$ apartments their home. Several residents were later identified as Soviet agents and the building was for many years under surveillance by the intelligence service. Now, following restoration, the gallery puts on exhibitions about the building and the artist community here. The flats themselves are private and can only be visited during the Open House event in September each year.

Lawn Road, NW3 2XD; isokongallery.org

Hampstead - Visit

④ Keats House
Home of the great Romantic poet

John Keats occupied this Regency villa in his final years, and at the height of his poetic powers. Despite suffering from tuberculosis, he penned *Ode to a Nightingale* here, and fell in love with Fanny Brawne, the 'beautiful, elegant, graceful, silly, fashionable and strange' girl next door. Their engagement was tragically brief – Keats died in Rome aged 25 – but relics of their love remain, like the almandine and gold ring he gave her. The house also commemorates Keats' literary friends with Leigh Hunt, Charles Lamb and William Hazlitt all featured. Once used by these men as a bachelor pad, the house eventually became Keats' sick room, evidence of which include his life and death masks and several posthumous portraits by his friend Joseph Severn, who devotedly nursed the poet in his last months in Rome. Poetry is still very much part of Keat's House today with an events programme featuring a high-profile poet in residence and a summer festival.

10 Keats Grove, NW3 2RR;
keatsfoundation.com

⑤ Kenwood House
Historic house on the heath

With its serene neo-Classical architecture, world-class picture collection, landscaped gardens and café, Kenwood is a favourite endpoint for many a Sunday afternoon walk through Hampstead Heath. The house is beautifully situated in 112 acres of parkland created by Sir Humphry Repton, and was remodelled for the 1st Earl of Mansfield by Robert Adam between 1764 and 1779. A major refurbishment in 2013 breathed new life into Kenwood's Adam interiors. The high point of this is the barrel vaulted Great Library; the gilded paintwork has been replaced by Adam's original colour scheme, a delicious confection of pale pink, blue and icing sugar white. The south front rooms have also been restored, their décor providing an elegant and sympathetic backdrop to Kenwood's big draw: the Iveagh Bequest of paintings. Bequeathed to the nation by the 1st Earl of Iveagh in 1927, this collection includes gems such as Rembrandt's late self-portrait and Vermeer's *Guitar Player*. There are frolicsome French paintings by Boucher, portraits by Van Dyck and plentiful works by British artists including Gainsborough, Reynolds and Romney. Three stately 20th-century sculptures can be admired in the grounds: *Two Piece Reclining Figure No.5* by Henry Moore, *Empyrean* by Barbara Hepworth and *Flamme* by Eugene Dodeigne. It's free to visit and has a café and shop, making it a great destination after time on the heath.

Hampstead Lane, NW3 7JR;
english-heritage.org.uk

Shop

❻ Borough Kitchen
Kitchen ware shop and cookery school
This branch of Borough Kitchen is the perfect place to get your kitchen ware. There's a lot of high-end cookware on offer here from Blenheim Forge knives to Staub cast iron pots, but there are also more modest items like linen tea towels and simple tableware for those with less cash to splash. If all these beautiful kitchen things inspire you to brush-up your cooking skill, the company also offers cookery courses from their kitchen next door.
1 Hampstead High Street, NW3 1RG;
boroughkitchen.com

❼ Flask Walk
Hampstead's famed alley
This alley was once where the citizens of Hampstead would draw water. These days you'll find a selection of independent shops and restaurants, as well as an historic pub dating from 1700. Chief among the shops is Keith Fawkes – a rare and second-hand bookshop that retains an old-world charm and is as much famed for it's antiques, that extend onto the pavement on sunny days. Meanwhile, Judy Green's Garden Store and Sayeh & Galton Flowers are here to help with all things horticultural.
14 Flask Walk, NW3 1HE

❽ Hampstead Community Market
Market in the heart of Hampstead
In operation for years and a throwback to less gentrified times, Hampstead Community Market has a butchers, fishmongers and greengrocers operating permanently, as well as a Saturday and Sunday market for craft goods and street food. The second-hand book stall is a favourite among Hampstead's literati, while the odd antique trader offers the opportunity for a bargain find. Minutes away from Hampstead tube station, it provides a good opportunity for picking up some picnic goods before making your way to the Heath.
78 Hampstead High Street, NW3 1RE

❾ Oxfam
Two of London's best charity shops
It is always a good idea to check out the charity shops in a prosperous area, as the donations are usually better quality. This rule definitely applies to the long-established Oxfam on Gayton Road where you are sure to find some great designer clothing, interesting homewares and of course (this being Hampstead) a great selection of books to sift through. If it's literature your after then the Oxfam Bookshop, further up the hill on Heath Street, is definitely worth a visit.
61 Gayton Road, NW3 1TU;
45 Heath Street, NW3 6UA

Hampstead - Eat & Drink

Eat & Drink

❿ The Duke of Hamilton
300 year old pub with a Jazz club beneath
Run by a local team and officially recognised as a community asset, this independent pub is worth seeking out. There's draft beer from Camden Town Brewery and a reasonable wine list, all served in an atmosphere that plays on the pub's long history. The old duke has plenty of space for dinning and their Sunday lunch is a firm favourite. The Hampstead Jazz Club has been running a busy programme in the basement since 2018 and is well worth checking out.

23-25 New End, NW3 1JD;
locipubs.com/duke

⓫ Giacobazzi's
Family-run Italian deli since 1991
This little-known spot is the best place for takeaway food near Hampstead Heath station. Everything from fresh pasta, charcuterie, pizza, focaccia, cakes and sandwiches are made on the premises each day. With so many green spaces nearby, this is a picnickers dream – think the best of Italian deli goods, including wine, olives and cheeses. Ditch the chains that choke up the high street for this family run spot, where the owner and his wife and children are always on hand to advise you as to what's best.

150 Fleet Road, NW3 2QX; giacobazzis.com

⓬ Ginger & White
A friendly local café and bakery
Hampstead can be a little hectic with busy roads transecting the village vibe. Tucked away in the charming pedestrian passageway of Perrins Court, G&W is a great place to relax and enjoy their delicious, freshly-made, cakes, sandwiches and coffee. They have some lovely treats on the menu like soft boiled eggs with soldiers and even fish finger sandwiches for those that want to indulge their guilty pleasures. The star of the show is definitely the Shakshuka that is a firm favourite with the locals. Outdoor seating makes this a perfect place to chill and watch the world go by and they also have a serving hatch for those that want to eat on the go.

4A-5A Perrins Court, NW3 1QS;
gingerandwhite.com

⓭ La Crêperie de Hampstead
The best crêpe in London
From a small kiosk outside the William IV pub, chef Edward de Mesquita has been offering delicious crêpes to the good folk of Hampstead since 1977. Over the years this little business has acquired quite a reputation and there are usually queues for their delicious sweet and savoury French pancakes and lots of celebrity fans. A definite must try in Hampstead.

77A Hampstead High Street, NW3 1RE;
lacreperiedehampstead.com

Hampstead - Outdoors

Outdoors

⑭ The Heath
Narnia of North London

Hampstead Heath feels like another world within London. An 800-acre expanse of woodland, meadows, ponds and hidden architectural wonders, there's very little you can't enjoy in London's largest ancient parkland. Many come for the swimming ponds, which have existed for hundreds of years and attract dedicated swimmers whatever the weather. Meanwhile, others enjoy picnicking, jogging or the view from Parliament Hill – arguably the best of London's skyline, so good in fact it's legally protected. At the bottom of the hill is an iconic Art Deco lido and athletics track, the former of which has a 61m unheated pool and a sauna which opens in the winter months. But really, you should come to the Heath first and foremost to wander amidst a landscape that retains a pastoral beauty rarely found elsewhere in London. The place inspired the poetry of Keats, the canvases of Constable and CS Lewis's *The Lion, The Witch and The Wardrobe*, so you're in good company. Look out for the Hill Garden and Pergola, a little-known neo-Georgian garden that is elegant yet charmingly untamed. Kenwood House looms over most of the Heath from its northern boundary, and is also well worth a visit (see p.71).
Heath Lodge, NW5 1QR; hampsteadheath.net

Stoke Newington

Stokey, as it's called by locals, is far older than the trendy restaurants and shops suggest. It has been a site of affluent residences since Tudor times, and really came to prominence in the 18th century, when Nonconformists settled here. Significant development has transformed this village from rural escape to architectural haven. In the 1960s and 70s squatters, artists and bohemians moved in and transformed Stokey into a place where radical politics thrived.

Today it's known for the wealthy who occupy the townhouses and enjoy the greenery and upmarket businesses. Chief among the attractions is Church Street, the aorta of Stokey, which thankfully today is largely car-fee, and is flanked with many places for pedestrians to eat and shop. At either end of the main strip are the lush Clissold Park and recently-revamped Abney Park. You could start by exploring either one of these green spaces before venturing along Church Street and perusing the many independent shops and eateries. Running perpendicular is the busy High Street, which has a handful of good shops to explore. You could also wander between the residential backstreets that run between the northern and southern boundaries of Woodbury Wetlands and Newington Green. Here you'll find what gives the neighbourhood its charm – a bucolic atmosphere characterised by preserved townhouses, local cafés and ample greenery – a postcard version of London.

STOKE NEWINGTON

1. Abney Park Cemetery
2. Castle Climbing Centre
3. St Mary's Old & New Church
4. Woodberry Wetlands & West Reservoir Centre (*off map*)
5. Church Street Bookshop
6. Growing Communities Farmers' Market
7. Hackney Flea Market
8. Kitchen Provisions
9. Meat N16
10. Know & Love
11. One Scoop Store
12. Retro Hub
13. Stoke Newington Bookshop
14. Stoke Newington Car Boot Sale (*off map*)
15. Yield N16 (*off map*)
16. Abney Park Café
17. Auld Shillelagh
18. Esters
19. Primeur (*off map*)
20. Rasa
21. Sonora Taqueria
22. Vicoli Di Napoli Pizzeria
23. Clissold Park

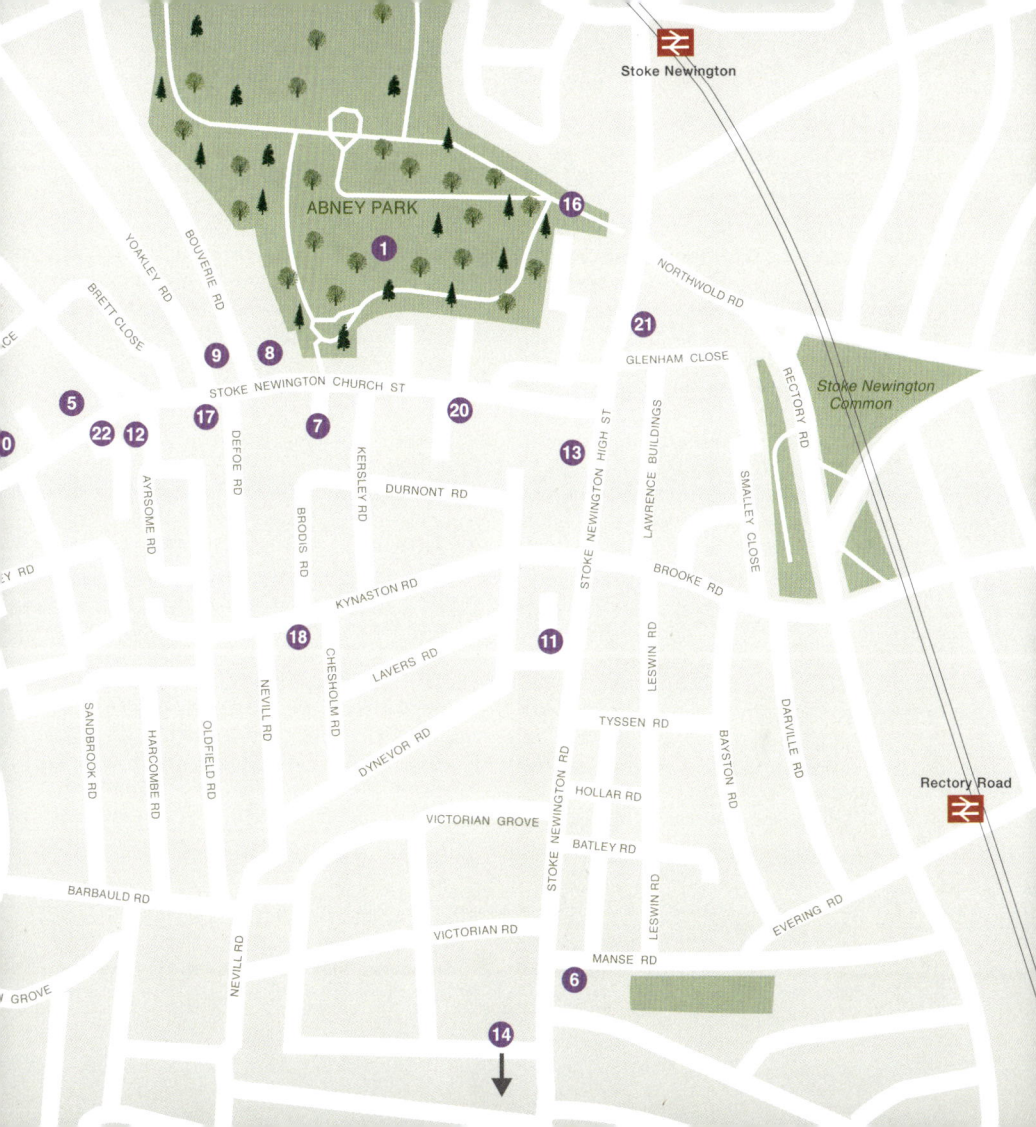

Visit

① Abney Park Cemetery
The first arboretum cemetery

It might seem macabre to introduce an area with a place of death, but this is no ordinary cemetery. Abney Park is one of the 'Magnificent Seven' London cemeteries, which are historically and ecologically important. Laid out in 1840, it became the chosen resting place for local Nonconformists. Start at the Egyptian-style ornamental iron gates, which lead past the newly refurbished park café (see p.92) and the old lodge that now serves as a children's environmental classroom. Passing the sundial, you'll find a spectacularly Gothic mess of tombstones and woodland, which is the largest in north London. Abney Park was the first arboretum to be combined with a cemetery in Europe. Its 2,500 trees and shrubs are labelled and arranged around the perimeter alphabetically, from A for Acer to Z for Zanthoxylum. Native oaks, ashes, elms and sycamores, as well as Hackney's sole surviving heathland, are some of the main natural attractions. Meanwhile, the graves are adorned with some of the grandest ornamental Victorian statuary. The most significant graves have detailed histories of their residents including the lion tamer Frank Bostock with his lion adorned grave. The recently-renovated chapel is another attraction with its newly installed artwork and remarkable stain-glass windows.

Stoke Newington High St, N16 0LH; abneypark.org

② Castle Climbing Centre
Bouldering within the battlements

It's hard to miss the seemingly random castle down Stokey's Green Lanes. The Grade II listed facility is in fact the most visited bouldering gym in Britain. Once a Victorian water pumping station, after becoming redundant in the 70s local campaigning saved it. Owing to its considerable stature – the tallest tower is more than 45m high – since 1995 it has been a go-to destination for top roping, lead climbing and auto-belay. It boasts 450 routes, as well as outdoor boulders in their organic garden. For people who can't get enough of the Castle, they offer yoga, massage therapy and more, as well as a shop and café. The Castle Climbing Centre is a unique community space that's open to all from skilled climbers to beginners.

Green Lanes, N4 2HA; castle-climbing.co.uk

Stoke Newington - Visit

❸ St Mary's Old & New Church
Two churches, one parish
The 'old' parish church dates from at least 1086, but the present Grade II* listed Elizabethan church, built in 1563, is one of the few remaining in the country and the only one in London. This old building is now a grassroots arts centre offering live music, art, poetry, dance and performance events in the evenings. The new church opposite is a much more imposing building that was completed in 1858 and is open during the day and has a little mobile coffee stall outside. The church has an impressive interior and is a good place to enjoy some calm on a day out here.
Stoke Newington Church Street, N16 9ES; stmaryn16.org

❹ Woodberry Wetlands & West Reservoir Centre
Inner-city wildlife sanctuary
It is fitting that Sir David Attenborough opened in this historic site to the public – Woodberry Wetlands is the premier inner-city wildlife sanctuary. The free-to-visit site is bedecked with a viewing boardwalk, visitor centre and café, as well as an abundance of keystone species. Lucky birdwatchers can spot some of Britain's rarer species such as kingfishers and warblers, while general enthusiasts can keep an eye out for bats, amphibians and insects. It's an equally fantastic place for volunteers looking to get hands-on experience with conservation. Visitors should keep in mind that no dogs other than registered assistance dogs are permitted. Next door, you'll find the West Reservoir Watersports Centre. Whether you're after sailing, kayaking or open-water swimming, it's a great place to take the kids on a day out, and adults can get involved too, or hang out in the café, housed in an old Victorian pumping station. Generally, booking in advance is required as, apart from swimming, the activities are run as instructed courses.
New River Path, Woodberry Grove, N16 5HQ; better.org.uk

Shops

❺ Church Street Bookshop
Long-established second-hand bookshop
Tim Watson set up this charming second-hand bookshop in 1994 and always has an interesting selection of fact and fiction to sift through. The shop offers anything from collectable hardbacks to well-thumbed paperbacks for just a few quid. The shop is only open Friday-Sunday (11am-5pm) but is always worth a browse.
146 Stoke Newington Church Street, N16 0JU

❻ Growing Communities Farmers' Market
UK's only all organic produce market
Growing Communities is the first and only 100% organic produce market in the UK, operating every Saturday from 10am to 2.30pm. As well as stalls selling all kinds of local, seasonal and sustainable veg, dairy and meat, there's an artisan French patissier and the fabulous mushroom stall that makes delicious sarnies. It's a pleasure to visit a market that has a real community spirit and is strongly supported by the locals who are often on first name terms with their favourite traders.
St Paul's Church, Stoke Newington Rd, N16 7UY; growingcommunities.org

❼ Hackney Flea Market
Antiquities by Abney cemetery
The Hackney Flea has quite the reputation. With 40 or so traders in a quaint town hall in the heart of the area, you can expect to find anything from vintage garden tools to posters and copper pans. There's lots of vintage clothing and jewellery, ranging from collectable trainers to authentic 1950s dresses. A tea & cake stall is on hand for when you need a pick me up after pottering between the paraphernalia. The event takes place one weekend a month, check the website for details.
Abney Hall,
73a Stoke Newington Church Street, N16 0AY; hackneyfleamarket.com

⑧ Kitchen Provisions
Emporium of kitchenware
Stokey's branch of Kitchen Provisions is well worth a detour for anyone after a high-quality knife, exquisite Japanese tools, or any well-made homeware. As ideal for buying gifts or kitting out your home, you can pick up a restaurant-standard kitchen knife for as little as £12, or a £4000 blade that wouldn't be out of place in a samurai movie or museum. Their knife-sharpening service is affordable, so you never need to wield a blunt instrument again.
92 Stoke Newington Church Street, N16 0LX; kitchenprovisions.co.uk

⑨ Meat N16
Butchers with their own book
This is the quality butcher of the neighbourhood, where you can get anything and everything meat, as well as some fantastic deli goods and wine. Pop in for a chat with the knowledgeable staff, some bones for the dog and sausages for tea. They're also much more than your average butcher, running lots of cookery courses and events for you to perfect your meat cooking and preparation skills. They've even made their own cookbook, so you can take more than just meat home with you.
104 Stoke Newington Church Street, N16 0LA; meatlondon.co.uk

🔟 Know & Love
Cavenous design shop
This two-tiered emporium is surprisingly large and airy, with an extensive selection of homeware, designer kitchenware, textiles, natural cosmetics and just about anything else you might need to brighten up your life. The green-fingered should definitely check out the little courtyard at the back of the shop, where the plants and utensils take centre-stage. One of the best things about Know & Love is their commitment to sourcing locally, with lots of great things from Hackney's designer-makers, including 3D-printed pots and Stokey-themed stationery and cards. A great store and one you'll definitely grow to know and love.
176 Stoke Newington Church Street, N16 0JL; knowandlove.co.uk

⓫ One Scoop Store
Great value vintage womenswear
This small but perfectly formed vintage shop punches well above its weight with a carefully curated selection of pre-loved and vintage womenswear. Holly founded the store back in 2017 after 15 years in the fashion industry and her eye for beautiful design is evident everywhere you look. The clothes are all well-presented and the prices are very reasonable, with a few discounted items to draw in the eagle-eyed bargain hunter. One Scoop is a store you should definitely go out of your way to visit.
101 Stoke Newington High Street, N16 0PH
onescoopstore.com

⓬ Retro Hub
Collectables in the heart of Stokey
This little yard off Stoke Newington Church Street has been selling second-hand gear and junk to the locals for decades. Places like this are not to everyone's taste but if you like searching for the odd treasure among the junk, this is a great place to roll up your sleeves and get stuck in. Inside it's much bigger than you think and there are lots of tempting bargains like a pristine Ercol sideboard for just £400 and a tatty but beautiful Chesterfield for only £200. It's a real gem and Jon and the team offer a great value delivery service within London.
2 Marton Road, N16 0RA;
retrohubn16.co.uk

⓭ Stoke Newington Bookshop
Long-running independent bookshop
This long-standing local favourite supplies readers from far and wide with both a broad selection of books and advice on recommended reads too. Just three doors down they also have a children's Toys and Books Shop, which is a must-visit for anyone with under 10s.
159 Stoke Newington High Street, N16 0NY;
stokenewingtonbookshop.co.uk

⓮ Stoke Newington Car Boot Sale
Old school boot sale
Car boot sales can be a little rough and ready, but this established event every weekend is one of the best. Think more 'retro' and less 'junk' with lots of regular traders bringing great collectables, furniture and artwork to this little school playground. If the bargain hunting makes you hungry, the organisers also run a little café serving the perfect car boot sale nosh – large mugs of tea and bacon sarnies.
Princess May School, N16 8DF;
londoncarboot.com

⓯ Yield N16
N16's natural wine know-it-alls
A wine merchant, deli and small bar stocking natural wines to buy or try alongside a menu of charcuterie and great local produce from Neal's Yard, e5 Bakehouse and more. Craft beer fans are taken good care of too. Great for learning more about wine thanks to the passionate staff, Yield is an important stop around a tour of Stoke Newington's shops. Check their website for regular events, including wine tastings.
44-45 Newington Green, N16 9PX;
yieldn16.com

Eat & Drink

🔴 Abney Park Café
Cemetery café
Opened as part of the recent revamp of the cemetery, this café fits in well with the surroundings, and makes for an ideal brunch stop, or just a cuppa while you explore the grounds or pass through the area. Local couple Lianna and Toby serve up breakfast dishes like french toast with seasonal fruit and toasties, and several salads at lunch, alongside all-day baked goods served from 8am until 4pm.
Abney Park, N16 0LH; abneyparkcafe.com

🔴 Auld Shillelagh
'Most authentic Irish pub outside Ireland'
Two titles are given to this boozer. First is 'most authentic Irish pub outside Ireland' by the Irish Times. Second is best pint of Guiness in London. A Stoke Newington stalwart, things stay lively here on account of the traditional music nights, a big beer garden for sunny days and sports on the telly when Ireland play, which always draws a crowd. The décor is very much that of a proper pub, with 'Off the leash and on the lash' the motto on their door frames. The timber beams sag as much as the locals come last orders, unless of course its St Patrick's Day, when a graveyard shift is to be expected. Prices are modest for the area, and the staff better craic than found at most Stokey pubs.
105 Stoke Newington Church Street, N16 0UD; theauldshillelagh.co.uk

Stoke Newington - Eat & Drink

⑱ Esters
If Bauhaus built a greasy spoon
If Bauhaus made a caff, this would be it. Forget overpriced avocado – Esters would be a dream to have on your doorstep. With a beautifully minimal interior that nods to the best-designed greasy spoons, it serves food that's equally refined – think international twists on a classic English brunch. In practice, this means you are as likely to have pork shoulder or confit duck as you are scrambled eggs. The seating fills up fast on weekends, and there are no reservations, but it's worth the wait. A no laptops policy stops it feeling like just another hipster hideout.
55 Kynaston Road, N16 0EB;
estersn16.com

⑲ Primeur
Team behind Westerns Laundry and Jolene
Situated in a converted early 20th century garage down an otherwise unassuming residential road, you'll know you're in the right place when you spot the original Barnes Motors façade. The daily-changing menu highlights British produce in bistro-style cooking – premium cuisine without pretension in the presentation. This, and their pioneering of natural wines, earned them both a Michelin Bib Gourmand and success at their subsequent spots, Westerns Laundry and Jolene bakery. Communal seating fills up fast, so book in advance to avoid disappointment.
Barnes Motors, 116 Petherton Road, N5 2RT;
primeurn5.co.uk

⓴ Rasa
Keralan curries in a technicolour restaurant

Think pink when you think Rasa – this Keralan restaurant stands out not just for its food, but also for the luminous hue of its façade. A local institution, its reputation comes from their vegetarian curries, served as platters on steel trays (thali), with a veritable rainbow of ingredients used. Mango, beets and bananas all feature in their curries, which are best enjoyed alongside appam – crispy rice pancake. Much of the food is vegan, and anything not containing ghee or paneer is clearly labelled. Rasa is also one of the more affordable eateries in the area.
55 Stoke Newington Church Street, N16 0AR; rasarestaurants.com

㉑ Sonora Taqueria
London's best taco spot

For a taste of Mexico, you only need to get the train to Stoke Newington. Sonora's tacos are homemade with corn, and packed full of barbecued pork or beef and salsas. You can enjoy these with other authentic flavours you'll struggle to find elsewhere, like micheladas, horchata and imported Mexican drinks. It's an exceedingly popular but tiny spot and currently just open Thursday to Sunday from midday until 4pm, so anticipate a queue. A couple from LA – the taco capital outside Mexico – attested Sonora was the real deal, giving it a chilli-coated thumbs-up! If the weather permits, consider enjoying your tacos in nearby Abney Park.
208 Stoke Newington High Street, N16 7HU; sonorataqueria.com

㉒ Vicoli Di Napoli Pizzeria
Second life of world-famous pizzeria

The Neapolitan-style pizza-only menu at Vicoli's has had hungry Londoners making a pizza pilgrimage there since its inception. The hype means you'll pay a bit of a premium, and there are limited tables, but a lunchtime or evening meal here is worth the trip. Beers and some desserts are also available, but the margherita is what you come for, executed perfectly. The cosy pizzeria also has a charming covered garden that's perfect when the weather is fine. If you're on the move and just fancy something on the go, their pizza wrap is perfect.
125 Stoke Newington Church Street, N16 0UH; vicolidinapoli.co.uk

Outdoors

㉓ Clissold Park
The biggest of Stokey's parks

The largest and best known of Stoke Newington's green spaces was once known as Crawshaw Farm, and only opened to the public in 1889. The 18th century Clissold House, which contains a café, is Grade II listed – along with the rest of the grounds. There is something to do for all interests and generations – the green is ideal picnic territory; young and old can hang out in the skate park and bowling green, respectively; animal lovers can check out the terrapin ponds, aviary and deer; kids can make a beeline for the playground and aspiring athletes make use of the many sports facilities. The summer months see the park packed full of sun-bathers and tennis enthusiasts, while winter provides equal solace for dog walkers and runners. Church Street and Green Lanes are nearby, so you're never far from a bus stop or train station, making Clissold Park a worthwhile stop on any Stokey itinerary.
Stoke Newington Church Street, N16 9HJ; clissoldpark.com

Islington

Once a source of water for the City of London, Islington took off in the 19th century as theatres and townhouses were built to attract the middle class. But soon the working poor, displaced by inner-city clearances, arrived, and overcrowding and poverty pervaded until after the Second World War. From the 1960s on, people have scrambled to buy Islington's Georgian terraces, and these well kept streets are often home to wealthy Londoners, especially those in politics and the media. If you'd like to get a feel for this history, follow the New River Path or Regent's Canal until you reach Upper Street, along which many of the attractions cluster. There are still several theatres to choose between, as well as galleries, shops and restaurants. A flavour of old Islington endures among the working-class traders on Chapel Market and the unique shops along Essex Road. Among the best of these is Mr Allsorts and Past Caring for collectables and vintage homeware, as well as Flashback Records for all your vinyl needs. There is also the picturesque Camden Passage that hosts one of London's last antiques and collectables markets. If you're in search of culture, hidden among the elegant townhouses are several local gems such as the Estorick Collection and Victoria Miro. If you need a break from the streets there are a few treasured green spaces such as Culpeper Community Garden – perfect places to catch your breath on a day out in Islington.

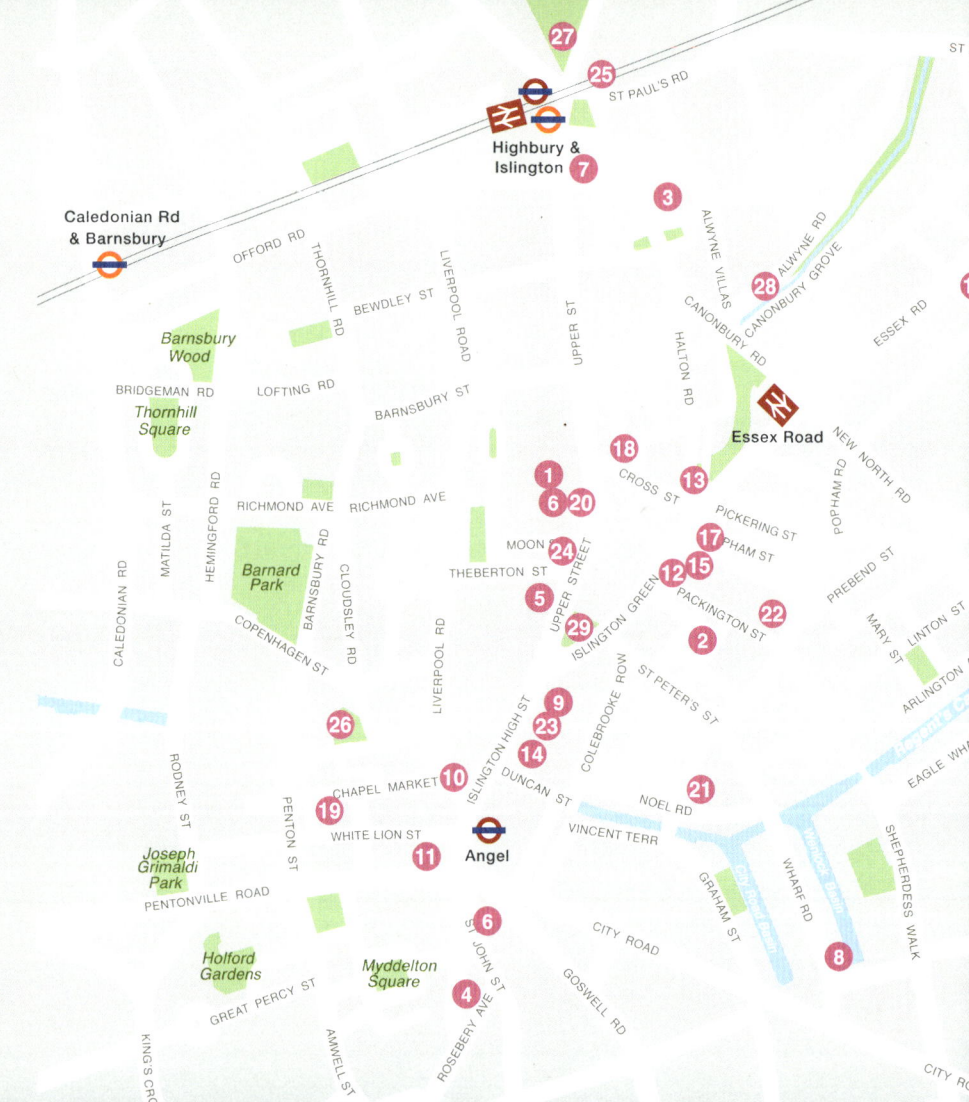

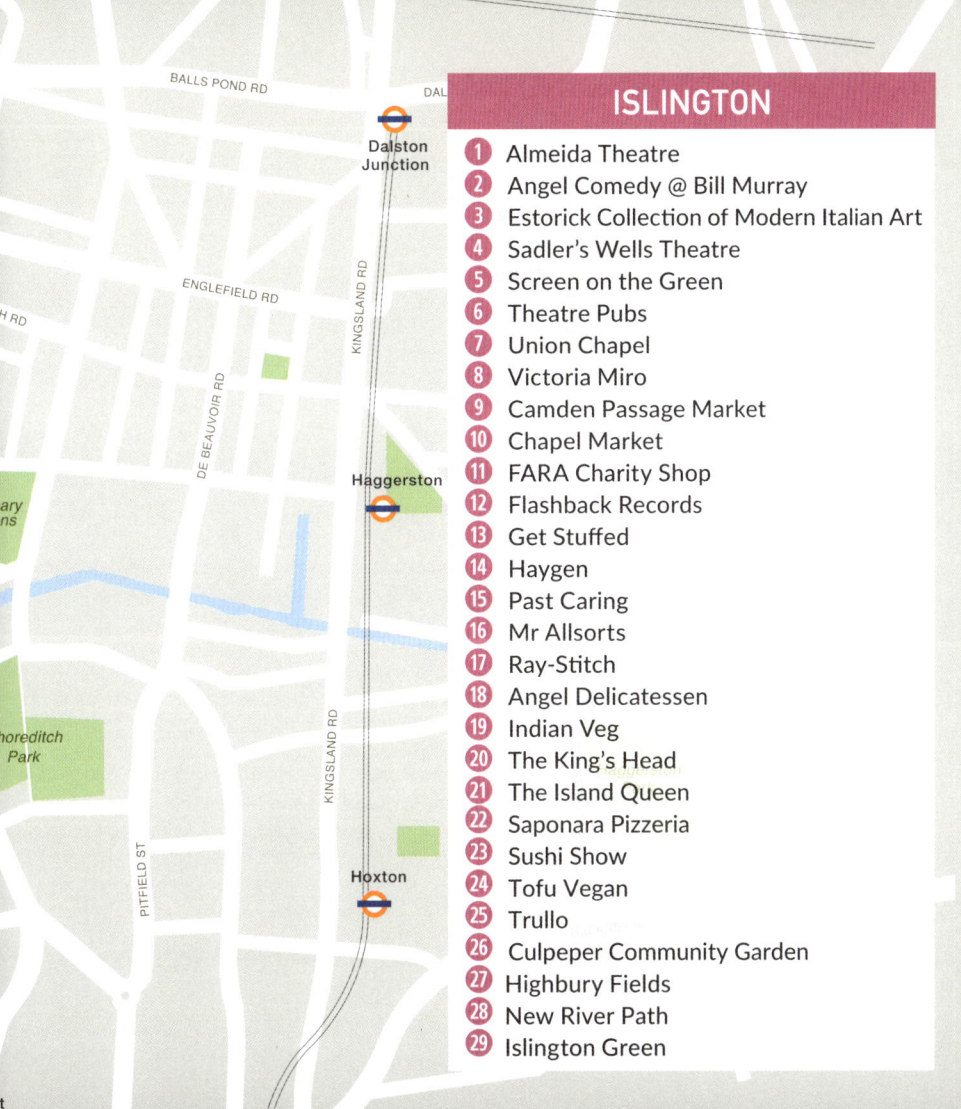

ISLINGTON

1. Almeida Theatre
2. Angel Comedy @ Bill Murray
3. Estorick Collection of Modern Italian Art
4. Sadler's Wells Theatre
5. Screen on the Green
6. Theatre Pubs
7. Union Chapel
8. Victoria Miro
9. Camden Passage Market
10. Chapel Market
11. FARA Charity Shop
12. Flashback Records
13. Get Stuffed
14. Haygen
15. Past Caring
16. Mr Allsorts
17. Ray-Stitch
18. Angel Delicatessen
19. Indian Veg
20. The King's Head
21. The Island Queen
22. Saponara Pizzeria
23. Sushi Show
24. Tofu Vegan
25. Trullo
26. Culpeper Community Garden
27. Highbury Fields
28. New River Path
29. Islington Green

Visit

❶ Almeida Theatre
Epicentre of Islington's 'enlightenment'
Although the Grade-II listed building dates to the 1830s, it wasn't until the 1980s that Almeida Theatre opened. Among the many composers and ensembles to perform here are Steve Reich, Philip Glass and John Cage. The Almeida has a reputation for fringe and avant-garde productions, including renowned performances of Harold Pinter's plays during the 1990s. Since then, it has attracted famous actors including Ralph Fiennes, Tilda Swinton and Benedict Cumberbatch to perform here while also enjoying Hollywood fame.
Almeida Street, N1 1TA; almeidatheatre.co.uk

❷ Angel Comedy @ The Bill Murray
Big names in comedy at laughably low prices
For big comedy names at laughably low prices, there's nowhere better than Angel Comedy. Originally operating from the Camden Head, their new pub venture at The Bill Murray has seen stars like Eddie Izzard, James Acaster and Stewart Lee share a stage with emerging talent and even the occasional first-timer. Between 20 and 30 shows run per week and there's a reasonably priced bar to add to the frivolity. The club also offers courses and community projects for those who want to try their hand.
39 Queen's Head Street, N1 8NQ;
angelcomedy.co.uk

❸ Estorick Collection
Futurist art in a Georgian townhouse
Futurist art is rare outside Italian galleries these days, what with its fascist connotations. But here, the works of progressive Italian artists like Balla, Severini and Boccioni form the beating heart of a unique collection, amassed by Eric and Salome Estorick after WWII. Opened in 1998 in a Georgian townhouse, you might mistake it for a grand Islington residence. But this domestic character makes the experience all the more exceptional. Futurist art forms the core of the collection, but other major 20th-century Italian artists are also represented, including de Chirico, Morandi, and Modigliani. A wonderful café in the glass conservatory is the icing on the cake of an unmissable Islington institution.
Northampton Lodge, 39a Canonbury Sq, N1 2AN;
estorickcollection.com

❹ Sadler's Wells Theatre
Most prolific dance theatre in the world
After centuries of both activity and dereliction, in 1926 Lilian Baylis helped revive Sadler's Wells and re-established its reputation for dance, drama and opera. Benjamin Britten worked here in the 1950s and Merce Cunningham was a regular visiting performer for a time. The current Grade II listed modern building dates to 1998 and contains a 1,500-seat auditorium. Sadler's Wells creates more new work than any other dance organisation, so there is always something of interest in their busy programme.
Rosebery Avenue, EC1R 4TN;
sadlerswells.com

❺ Screen on the Green
20th-century fleapit now a famous cinema
The Screen on the Green is one of the UK's oldest cinemas, having opened in 1913, and is instantly recognisable with its red neon façade. In the 1970s it became famous when the then owner, Romaine Hart, started inviting bands to perform including The Sex Pistols, The Clash and The Buzzcocks. She also turned the old fleapit into an arthouse cinema, showing cult films like *Eraserhead* and *This is Spinal Tap*. The cinema has been renovated since those radical days and is now part of the Everyman group, but still offers an interesting programme of independent films and the occasional block buster.
83 Upper Street, N1 0NP;
everymancinema.com

❻ Theatre Pubs
A place for a pint and a play
Theatre pubs are a unique phenomenon to these isles, and Islington has its fair share. The King's Head at 115 Upper Street is the oldest operating one in the UK, open since 1970, although the theatre has now moved to its own site behind the pub with its own entrance. Meanwhile, the Old Red Lion is one of the oldest pubs in the UK, having first been built in 1415 (and now Grade II listed). At both venues, you'll find a proper pub interior at the front where you can enjoy a drink before or after the show. Tickets start from £10.
Islington Square, 116 Upper Street, N1 1QN ;
418 St John Street, EC1V 4NJ

Islington - Visit

❼ Union Chapel
Venue with award-winning acoustics
Alongside its clerical work, this Grade-I listed 19th-century Gothic revival church hosts live entertainment in aid of local homeless people. With 250 or so events a year spanning film, music and comedy, and some of the best acoustics in town, this is has become an award-winning venue. The most spectacular feature of the chapel is the organ, which was designed by Henry Willis in 1877, the foremost organ builder of the Victorian era. Take a look at their website to find out about forthcoming events.
19b Compton Terrace, N1 2UN,
unionchapel.org.uk

❽ Victoria Miro
C'est chic gallery
Victoria Miro c'est chic – understated in presentation, and contrasted with the boldest of the exhibitions. It's known for consistently curating unforgettable shows in a 8,000-square-foot former Victorian furniture factory. They represent established names like Turner Prize winners Chris Ofili and Grayson Perry, alongside trailblazers such as Milton Avery and Howardena Pindell. Arguably the star of the show is the landscaped garden. Swans glide past as you wander between outdoor sculptures by the likes of Yayoi Kusama, creating a slice of paradise in an otherwise industrial corner of Islington.

16 Wharf Road, N1 7RW; victoria-miro.com

Shop

❾ Camden Passage Market
Arcadia for antiques

Not actually in Camden, this discreet pedestrianised street is lined with antique dealers, and with its flagstone paving has an old-world feel in contrast to the modern shops of Upper Street. The buildings are a mix of Victorian and Edwardian, but the market started in the 1960s, as part of the gentrification that has seen Islington become one of London's most sought-after neighbourhoods. Visit on Wednesdays or Saturdays for the full experience – you'll find vintage stalls accompanying the shops, so you can flit between bric-à-brac for a few quid to genuine objets d'art for several hundred pounds. The best stalls congregate around the Camden Head pub, while some of the smarter shops are found at the opposite end of the passage. Also at this part of the market and not to be missed is Pierrepont Arcade, a covered area with al fresco stalls and an indoor maze of units selling smaller collectables like stamps and medals. Camden Passage is one of the big four antiques markets in London, along with Bermondsey, Portobello Road and Covent Garden, and is always worth a visit.

Camden Passage, N1 8EA;
camdenpassageislington.co.uk

❿ Chapel Market
The last of the old Islington
Chapel Market has been around since 1870 and is one of the last links left to the old working-class identity of Islington that has been swallowed up by gentrification. It feels very different to much of the surrounding area, with a real sense of community evident in the many traders chatting away to their regular customers. It's easy enough to do your entire weekly shop here, with the usual suspects like a deli van, vendors selling fruit, veg, fresh meat and fish, alongside stalls where you'll find everything from flowers and haberdashery to beds and phones. Don't miss the bargain bike parts trader too. Barry the fishmonger has been selling here for 30 years, while John the fruit and veg man has worked here since he was a kid in 1974. You'd be hard-pressed to find a place with more character and characters in London.
Chapel Market, N1 9EN

⓫ FARA Charity Shop
Famed charity shop
Close to Angel tube station, this huge charity shop has a reputation that draws in thrift shoppers from across the capital. Expect to find rail upon rail of fashion from designer labels to basic high street names. The prices are reasonable and there are always discount rails and bins for those looking for a real bargain. This FARA is a legendary charity shop and always a good first port of call on a visit to Islington.
28-32 Pentonville Road, N1 9HJ

⓬ Flashback Records
MVP for music industry insiders
A favourite spot for DJs and producers, Flashback has an exceptionally well-catalogued collection of vintage records. Outside you'll find bargain boxes, and upstairs you'll find CDs of every genre, but it's the basement's library that demands immediate attention. Admittedly, you can trawl their website for any missing gems in your collection, but a good rummage in person is bound to dig up some gold. Jazz, soul, hip-hop and dance all vie for space, and as it's all second-hand, you can expect to find a few bargains.
50 Essex Road, N1 8LR;
flashback.co.uk

⓭ Get Stuffed
Shop giving a second life to animals
Unless you're in the market for taxidermising your old dog, you might not have much reason to visit this appropriately named shop. Wander past, and that might just change – onlookers are promised the most intriguing window-shopping experience in all of London. Lions, giraffes and bears will meet your gaze with a death stare. The Sinclair family business has been stuffing ethically-sourced animal corpses (provided by zoos only after an animal dies) on the premises for over 40 years. The shop operates under the strictest regulations, so, if you happen to have a furry friend you'd like to preserve for posterity, this is the place to come. Otherwise it remains an oddity that is worth visiting for the spectacle.
105 Essex Road, N1 2SL;
thegetstuffed.co.uk

⓮ Haygen
Skandi style in the heart of Islington
This stylish gift shop at the end of Camden Passage is always worth a browse. Modern graphic art, jewellery, women's fashion and cards and stationery are all part of the offering. The shop itself is a lesson in simple skandi style with its white walls, parquet flooring and a large glass shop front. Haygen is a great place to find gifts or just a bit of self care with a selection of cosmetics, balms and perfumes.
114 Islington High Street, N1 8EG;
haygenshop.com

Islington - Shop

⓯ Past Caring
Haven of kitsch paraphernalia
Another aptly named speciality shop on Essex Road, this emporium of retro goods is anything but unloving towards its stock of 1970s furniture, glassware, ceramics and clothing. A haven of kitsch paraphernalia, you'll also find books, fabrics and bric-à-brac, all genuine articles and presided over by the expert owners. In operation since 1973, this has been a long-time go-to for Islington locals looking to brighten up their homes, but even as gentrification has witnessed prices everywhere rising, here they've been kept down to earth.
54 Essex Road, N1 8LR

⓰ Mr Allsorts
Aladdin's Cave of collectables
Mr Allsorts and his trusty canine companion, Emilio, have been selling bric-à-brac and collectables from this corner shop at the far end of Essex Road for decades. The shop front might seem relatively small but beyond the threshold there's a surprising amount of interesting stock to sift through. On fine days the larger items like sofas and tables extend onto the street where both man and dog can enjoy the sunshine and chat with their friends. It's a great place to find a bargain and one well worth seeking out.
191 Northchurch Road, N1 3NT

⓱ Ray-Stitch
Sewing, knitting and so much more
For those who enjoy sewing or knitting this stylish haberdashers is a wonderful place to visit with its bewildering range of fabrics, ribbons, lace and threads. There are all kinds of accessories from thimbles to buttons, tape measures and pins of every kind. If you feel your skills need improving they also run classes for every level and the staff are always on-hand to offer support and advice.
66-68 Essex Road, N1 8LR, raystitch.co.uk

Eat & Drink

⑱ Angel Delicatessen
A favourite local café
This little café and deli is easily missed, but well worth seeking out. The business has been through several hands over the years but is now run with friendly efficiency by Rozanna, who continues to offer freshly made Italian fare and excellent coffee. There are tables outside, but these are hard to get with a loyal clientele guaranteed to show up on fine days. The only drawback to this lovely local is the limited opening times (12-5pm).
48 Cross Street, N1 2BA

⑲ Indian Veg
Cheap-as-chips curry
This buffet offers cheap as chips curries where you can indulge with its all-you-can-eat offering for a few quid. It's always popular with locals who often queue at lunchtime. Costs are further kept down by the bring your own booze policy, although the propaganda posters covering the walls discourage drinking, meat-eating and just about every other distraction from spiritual pursuits. It does make for a unique dining atmosphere – not that decor matters when you've got platefuls of bhajis and parathas in front of you. An old-school Islington institution.
92-93 Chapel Market, N1 9EX

⑳ The King's Head
Theatrical pub on Upper Street
There are quite a few pubs to choose from along Upper Street, but the King's Head has bags of character and a friendly atmosphere that makes it stand out. The character comes from its long history as a theatre pub, with pictures of famous thespians on the wall, as well as posters from former shows. There's a good wine list and the pub also offers cheese and charcuterie to accompany your tipple of choice. The pub is part of the Youngs group but has managed to keep its unique atmosphere, despite the theatre moving to its own purpose-built venue on Islington Square.
115 Upper Street, N1 1QN;
kingsheadtheatre.com

㉑ The Island Queen
Friendly local just off the canal
When so many local, neighbourhood pubs are closing down, The Island Queen has adapted to survive with its Victorian exterior now painted in muted green, the large windows clear glass and the interior a model of relaxed urban chic. The beers on tap are all from the likes of Hammerton Brewery, Thornbridge and Beavertown and they have a reasonable wine list and cocktails for those who have something to celebrate. The pub also does great Mediterranean inspired bar snacks and a more hearty sit-down menu. Close to the canal and surrounded by some of Islington's smartest terraces, The Island Queen is definitely worth seeking out.
87 Noel Road, N1 8HD;
theislandqueenislington.co.uk

㉒ Saponara Pizzeria
Authentic Italian off the beaten track
Saponara has been serving delicious Italian food and selling authentic produce for decades and has acquired quite a reputation and a loyal following. It's a little bit of a trek from the main Islington high street, but it's worth it for some of the best pizza in London and freshly made pasta, all at reasonable prices. It's times vary a little, so best to check before making a special journey.
23 Prebend Street, N1 8PF;
saponarapizzeria.co.uk

㉓ Sushi Show
Show stopping sushi
This small sushi joint punches way above its weight with a fabulous selection of freshly prepared sushi that never disappoints. Great sushi depends on the freshest fish and founder, Kaz Tateishi, has been a fish supplier for over 25 years, making sure that only the best is used for his sushi. The business is largely geared around take-out but there are outside tables if you want to enjoy a sit down treat. If there's no room to eat-in, get a tray and enjoy an alfresco sushi snack on Islington Green (see p.117).
28 Camden Passage, N1 8ED;
sushishowlondon.com

㉔ Tofu Vegan
The go-to vegan Chinese restaurant
Tofu Vegan is the go-to vegan Chinese restaurant. It is easier to find good Chinese food now, but here you're really spoilt for choice. Nine different dumplings, lotus leaf buns and cucumber salads accompany tofu transformed into succulent vegan chicken or sizzling plant-based pork. If you don't fancy imitation meat, then there are dishes like cloud ear fungus or fried king oyster mushrooms that show how vegetables can be king. Dessert consists of things with sweet bean or lotus seeds. In the years since opening, Tofu Vegan has already branched out – a testament to their popularity. The interiors are plain, which lets the food do the talking and the prices very reasonable.
105 Upper Street, N1 1QN; tofuvegan.com

㉕ Trullo
A slice of Italy in Islington
Named after the conical stone houses in Puglia that are now a UNESCO World Heritage Site, Trullo is a place you'd like to call home. From the people behind Padella (see Borough p.205) comes an upmarket sister restaurant that dishes up seasonal British produce as antipasti, pasta, secondi and puddings galore. Pappardelle with beef shin ragu is unmissable, as is their T-bone steak to share and the Amalfi lemon tart. The wine list is on the expensive side, so save this sophisticated spot for a special occasion lunch or go with friends and spread the cost.
300-302 St Paul's Road, N1 2LH;
trullorestaurant.com

Islington - Eat & Drink

Outdoors

㉖ Culpeper Community Garden
Bombsite turned secret garden
Transformed by the community for the community, this triangular plot of land was once a Blitz-era bombsite, but now brims with plants and buzzes with wildlife, a verdant oasis of urban Islington. The layout is a model of clever planning: serpentine paths weave around the garden, giving the space a Tardis-like expansiveness. Rock gardens run adjacent to picnic lawns, herbariums, as well as frog-filled ponds and allotment plots. Events include live music, gardening workshops, talks and plant sales.

1 Cloudesley Road, N1 0EJ;
culpeper.org.uk

㉗ Highbury Fields
Picture perfect park in the heart of Highbury
At just over 11 acres, Highbury Fields is Islington's biggest open space. As well as parkland, it contains tennis courts and Highbury Pool. The surrounding Georgian and Victorian townhouses are picture-perfect in their preservation, and correspondingly are some of the most expensive residences in London. At the south end stands a statue commemorating less fortunate residents that lost their lives in the Boer War.

Highbury Crescent, N5 1AR

㉘ New River Path
Ancient waterway and modern walking trail
Built in 1613 as an aqueduct by Sir Hugh Myddelton (whose statue is on Islington Green), the New River Path provides an amenable, waymarked walking route from New Gauge, Hertford, through the Lee Valley and three London boroughs before hitting Islington. Here, it emerges for a stretch to provide a lush oasis amid the urban surroundings. Enter from Canonbury Grove to enjoy a stroll by the river, and perhaps stop for a pint at the nearby Marquess Tavern.

Canonbury Grove, N1 2HP

㉙ Islington Green
Green island amid the traffic
Islington is relatively thin on the ground when it comes to parks, so this patch of green at the junction between Upper Street and Essex Road provides a much valued public space amid the busy streets. Even on sunny days you can find a picnic spot or bench to enjoy your lunch. Notable features include a modern war memorial by John Maine that was installed in 2007. At the apex of the park look out for the corroded stone monument to Sir High Myddleton, who brought water to the village of Islington over 400 years ago and helped make the borough what it is today.

Islington Green, N1 0NP

East

Hackney
Shoreditch
Walthamstow

Hackney

Today, it's hard to imagine Hackney was once a rural village outside London. There are just a few remnants of the area's ancient past, but development from the Georgian and Victorian periods stands out. The architecture is in part why Hackney has gentrified so quickly: the large, well-built townhouses are now some of the most sought after in London. To some, the area is synonymous with hipsters, and the influence of affluent consumers is easy to see. But not all of this is bad and the area is a far cry from the dystopian vision of Martin Amis' *London Fields*. The neighbourhood is now awash with great markets, shops and restaurants, so there's always more than enough to do. Broadway Market in particular is a life giving artery for the area, attracting a steady stream of bright young things who enjoy its pubs, restaurants and shops. Saturday (and now Sunday) is best, as the market is in full swing, but any day is worthwhile, especially as London Fields is just next door. Many attractions are found on nearby Mare Street too, but best of all is Victoria Park – East London's answer to Hyde Park – which will easily keep you satisfied with a day of wandering, easily accessed via a leisurely stroll down Regent's Canal.

HACKNEY

1. Hackney Empire
2. Hackney Museum
3. London Fields Lido
4. Lychee One
5. MOTH Club
6. Netil House
7. SPACE
8. The Last Tuesday Society
9. Broadway Market
10. Broadway Bookshop
11. Burberry Outlet
12. Lauriston Village
13. Paper Dress Vintage
14. Somewhere in Hackney
15. Café Cecilia Climpson & Sons
16. Climpson & Sons
17. E5 Bakehouse
18. Hill & Szrok
19. Koya Ko Hackney
20. OMBRA
21. pockets
22. Victoria Park Market
23. London Fields
24. Regents Canal
25. Victoria Park

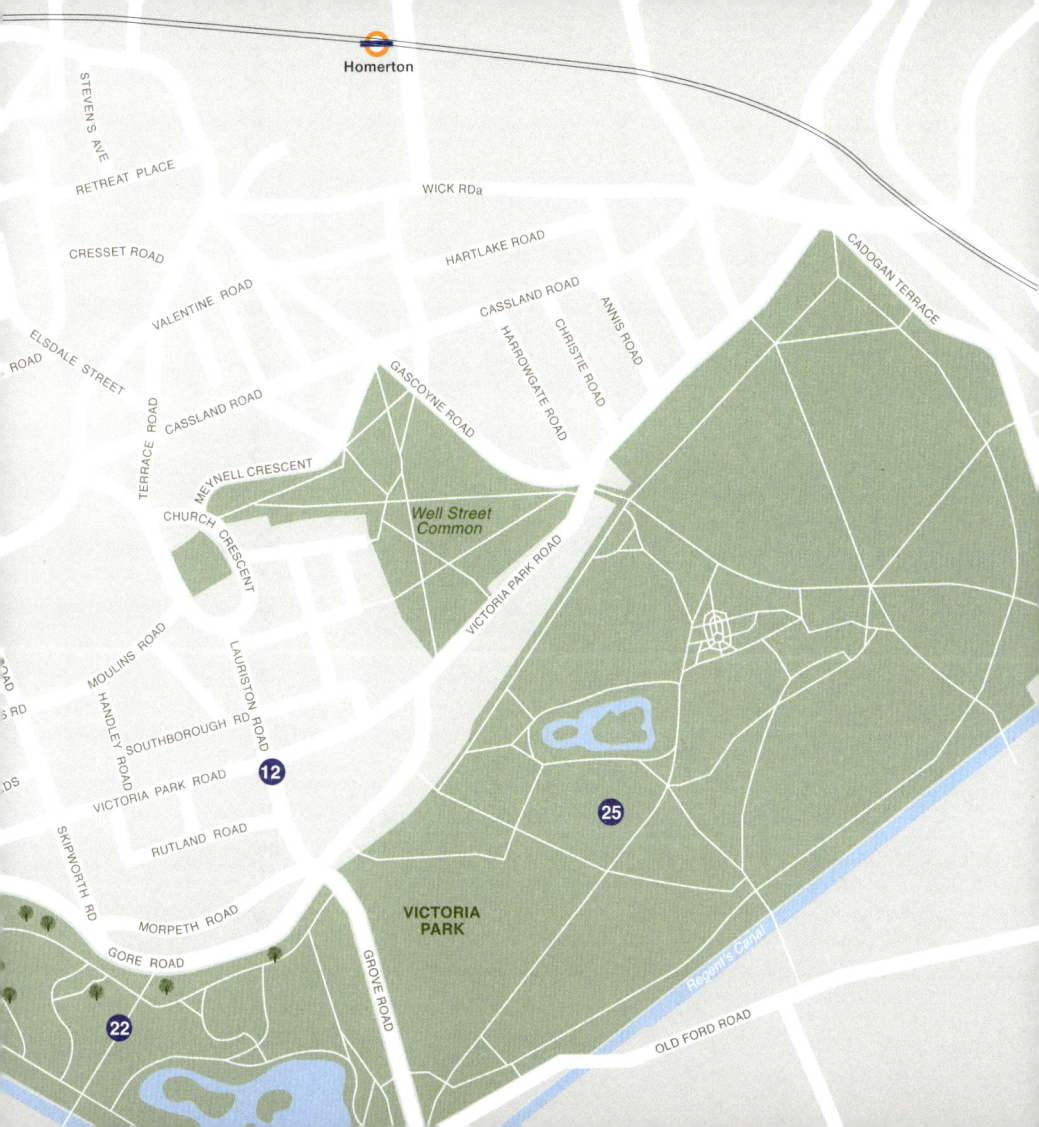

Visit

❶ Hackney Empire
A powerhouse of performing arts
Unparalleled for its grandeur in this part of Hackney, the Empire theatre has paid host to some of the biggest names in British entertainment over its long history, from Charlie Chaplin to Ralph Fiennes and Lenny Henry. It has been a music hall, theatre and comedy arena over the years, but now does all three. The Empire also has a restaurant and bar to enjoy a pre-show drink or meal and make an evening of any event.
291 Mare Street, E8 1EJ;
hackneyempire.co.uk

❷ Hackney Museum
Unsung stories in unseen spaces
You might not expect such depth of history in a local library, but Hackney is no ordinary borough. Focusing on migration, settlement and the area's rich diversity, you can trace stories from the Roman period right through to the present day. Many will be surprised to place Hackney's cultural scene in the struggles and triumphs of communities decades ago, told through the artwork of BAME and LGBT groups. There are talks, plenty for kids to interact with and free entry – this really is one of the neighbourhood's best-kept secrets.
1 Reading Lane, E8 1GQ;
hackney-museum.hackney.gov.uk

❸ London Fields Lido
London's most loved open-air pool
Originally built in 1931, London Fields Lido was closed in the mid-80s and left to rot until after years of campaigning it was revamped and reopened in 2006. It is now one of Hackney's greatest assets, offering a beautiful 50m outdoor pool that is kept at a pleasant 25C. In recent years flood lighting has been added so committed swimmers can enjoy a paddle after dark. The café kiosk sells good coffee, flapjacks and falafel wraps for a post-workout fix. Little wonder it's the city's most visited lido.
London Fields, E8 3EU; better.org.uk

❹ Lychee One
Eastern eccentricities, Western weirdness
Easy to miss but worth tracking down, this emerging exhibition space focuses on abstract, Avant-garde sculpture and painting. They occasionally host provocative performance pieces too, which draws in the nearby art school crowd. Lychee One describes itself as a meeting point for Eastern and Western artists, founder Lian Zhang being the first Chinese woman to open a contemporary art gallery in London. Their commercial ventures are particularly approachable – works on their website start from as little as £5.
Unit 1, The Gransden,
39-45 Gransden Avenue, E8 3QA;
lycheeone.com

⑤ MOTH Club
Glitz and glam meets the working man
With glitz and glam from floor to ceiling, you'd be hard-pressed to find a less typical working men's club than this. MOTH Club – or The General Browning Memorable Order of Tin Hats Club – is an ex-Servicemen's members club that is now one of the hottest multi-events spaces in town. You're as likely to find talks by Will Self, comedy sets by Romesh Ranganathan or secret shows thrown by Lady Gaga and Mark Ronson under the golden vaults. Some of the original club's features are still to be seen, including the 'ALL CHILDREN TO BE OFF THE DANCEFLOOR BY 9.30PM' plaque. The spirit of the old club is still kept alive with popular quizzes, cabaret nights and film screenings.
Old Trades Hall, Valette Street, E9 6NU;
mothclub.co.uk

⑥ Netil House
Beauty in the brutal
This tower block by London Fields is the residence for a creative community of 600+ artisans and businesses. With on-site spaces including a rooftop bar, café, restaurant, salon, work studios and neighbouring market; there isn't much missing for visit here. Host to regular free events too, DJs create the ambience for open artists' studios, sample sales and after parties thrown till late. The rooftop vista is a highlight, offering a rare 360-degree view of an industrial East London cityscape.
1 Westgate Street, E8 3RL;
netil360.com

⑦ SPACE
A small step for art-kind
Though SPACE is low-profile, their charitable & creative outreach spans across London's boroughs, providing studios for emerging artists and projects in local schools. It's little wonder considering they're the oldest artist studio organisation in town and helped start the East End's cultural renaissance. Their Hackney outpost offers more than enough by way of contemporary & experimental multimedia art, having shown names like Jo Spence, Kathy Acker and Nam June Paik. Come prepared for the weird and wonderful and look out for the free exhibitions that are a regular feature here.
129-131 Mare Street, E8 3RH;
spacestudios.org.uk

⑧ The Last Tuesday Society / Viktor Wynd Museum of Curiosities
The Horniman in a Hackney basement
The Last Tuesday Society is London's most unusual bar, run with eclectic and eccentric gusto by the remarkable Viktor Wynd. The bar boasts the UK's most extensive absinthe list, and an atmosphere that is part Baudelaire, part Nick Cave. But take the Museum of Curiosities' staircase and watch reality turn 'pataphysical'. Floor to ceiling, there's all manner of taxidermy, including the skeleton of conjoined twins, Papua New Guinean tribal masks and an itinerant reptilian petting zoo. Your cup of tea? Keep an eye peeled on their calendar.
11 Mare Street, E8 4RP; lasttuesdaysociety.org

Shop

⑨ Broadway Market
One of east London's great markets

If there is one thing you choose to do in London Fields, it ought to be visiting Broadway Market. Asides from historic and cultural significance, it is simply the aorta of the area with all kinds of opportunities to shop, eat and drink. The street, flanked by London Fields on one side and Regents' Canal on the other, has seen an array of traders since the 1890s, but the current iteration is arguably the most bustling. The market is best-known for its mix of clothing boutiques like Retrouvé and arty bookshops such as Donlon Books and Artwords. If you're after a wider selection of reading material there's nowhere better than Broadway Bookshop. There are also posh delis like L'eau á La Bouche, several raucous pubs and of course, the Weekend Market. The market offers great new & second-hand clothes, arts and craft, bookstalls, fresh artisanal produce and some of London's best street food. Sea urchins and samosas vie for attention amid a steady stream of punters, and from top to bottom the street hums with the sound of live music and the energy of people having a good time.

Broadway Market, E8 4QJ;
broadwaymarket.co.uk

Hackney - Shop

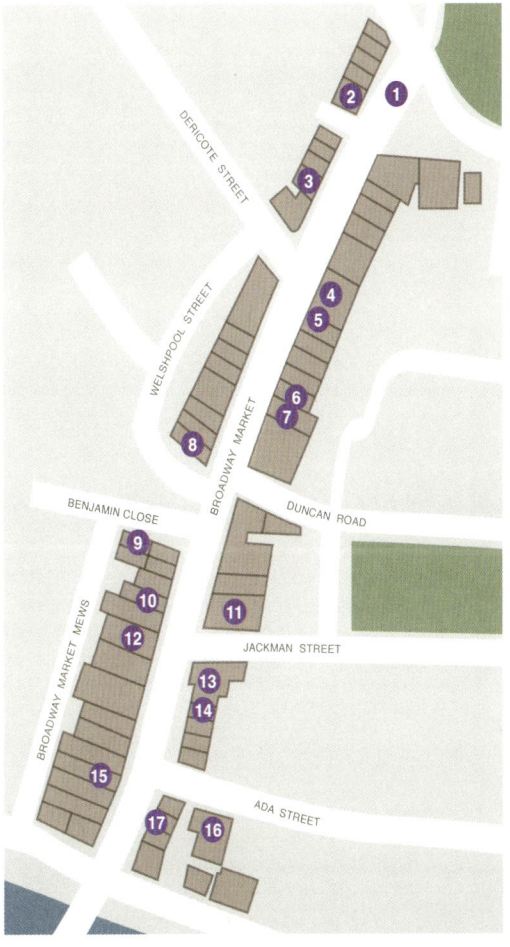

1. Weekend market
2. Donlon Books
3. Climpson & Sons Café
4. Aya & Suki
5. Hill & Szrok Master Butcher & Cookshop
6. Franca Manca
7. Buen Ayre
8. L'eau á La Bouche deli
9. Koya Ko
10. Shrine to the Vine
11. The Dove
12. Retrouvé
13. Artwords Bookshop
14. Pavilion Bakery
15. Fabrications
16. House of Vintage
17. Broadway Bookshop

Hackney - Shop

❿ Broadway Bookshop
The ideal independent bookshop
Independent bookshops are an increasingly rare breed these days, but Broadway Bookshop is bucking the trend by thriving at the far end of the busy market street. As the idiom goes, don't judge a book by its cover. What initially appears to be a small shop actually stretches back with floor-to-ceiling shelves on all walls stocking an impressive selection of titles, especially the latest works by acclaimed writers. The knowledgeable staff are on-hand to help you find something specific, but if you pop in for a browse, you are bound to emerge with a new book in your hand.
6 Broadway Market, E8 4QJ;
broadwaybookshophackney.com

⓫ Burberry Outlet
Designer labels in Hackney's back streets
There has been a Burberry Outlet on this quiet Hackney street for many years. It's a large and rather smart ground level showroom that manages to draw designer bargain hunters from around the world. For a while the success of Burberry in Hackney drew in a number of high value names such as Aquascutum and Nike. These rival outlets have all closed in recent years, leaving Burberry as the stand-out attraction. The sight of wealthy Chinese tourists arriving by taxi from their west end hotels to this Hackney back street is something to behold.
29-31 Chatham Place, E9 6LP

⑫ Lauriston Village
A lesson in local living
Lauriston Road (from Victoria Park Road to Victoria Park) offers an escape from nearby crowds of Broadway Market and a distinctly neighbourhood feel. The small cluster of independent shops and cafés is a welcome alternative to the identikit High Street. One shop that stands out is Sublime for designer clothes and gifts. If it's quality food you're after there's a Ginger Pig butchers, Jonathan Norris Fishmongers and the Deli Downstairs, as well as Bottle Apostle for fine wine. Eateries include Bruno's Wine Bar and a branch of Pophams, whose cardomon buns are the stuff of dreams. There's even a branch of Gail's – a sure sign that this is one of the swankiest parts of Hackney.
Lauriston Road, E9 7HJ

⑬ Paper Dress Vintage
Nothing flimsy about their fashion
Too often, vintage is a lazy excuse: grubby clothes for naïve shoppers in London's lacklustre chains. Praise be to Paper Dress Vintage, those arbiters of proper period fashion. Their garments eclipse the 1920s to 80s – you'll be hard pressed to find better. Genuine kimonos, embroidered kaftans and all manner of cotton dresses fill the boutique's two floors. After dark, Paper Dress blossoms into a bar and live music venue, featuring open mic sessions, Swing gigs and Lynchian rock nights. If we can't sell it to you, they surely can.
352a Mare Street, E8 1HR;
paperdressvintage.co.uk

⑭ Somewhere in Hackney Vintage
Women's fashion underneath the arches
Previously operating under a neighbouring archway, this vintage emporium is the lovechild of proprietor Melanie, who for years has sold Hackney residents the best of women's fashion. She has a loyal following who come to her for expert curation and advice, as well as affordable prices. Whatever sort of occasion you're shopping for, Somewhere in Hackney is worth seeking out. Mel's Instagram @somewhereinhackney is a great resource with all her latest finds to check out before a visit.
394 Mentmore Terrace, E8 3PH;
somewhereinhackney.com

Eat & Drink

⓯ Café Cecilia
Irish-inspired fine dining
When chefs from celebrated restaurants open their own place, parallels are almost always drawn. Max Rocha's Café Cecilia is no different. Stints at St JOHN and the River Cafe are evident in the somewhat Spartan interior and menus, that let the cooking stand out. The dishes are fun, and it's USP is Irish cuisine at the highest level. Guinness bread ice cream, or Guinness bread with your kippers? Many dishes aren't strictly Irish. You can enjoy great pasta here, as well steak & chips and deep-fried bread & butter pudding. Booking is advised, although some space is saved for walk-ins.
32 Andrews Road, E8 4FX; cafececilia.com

⓰ Climpson & Sons
Broadway's artisanal brunch bolthole
Climpson and Sons' original 1915 façade makes it look like they've always been here, but they were part of the first wave of gentrification that hit Hackney in the 90s. Here, coffee geeks are welcome to choose between brewing methods and 8 varieties of in-house roasts, sourced from farms globally. You may have enjoyed their coffee already as they supply many of London's best independent cafés. Pastries and savoury brunch dishes are also available to accompany your caffeine fix.
67 Broadway Market, E8 4PH;
climpsonandsons.com

⑰ E5 Bakehouse
The borough's best bakery

Occupying three cavernous railway arches near London Fields station, E5 Bakehouse is to many the best bakery in the borough. Their success ensures that everything here is freshly made, with their electric delivery bike a common sight as it transports their legendary sourdough loaves and artisanal pastries to establishments far and wide. In-house, they offer delicious European-style brunches and their grocery shop at the front counter is zero-waste. As well as quality food there is hand-thrown porcelain and classic utensils to inspire your home-cooking. They also run masterclasses on bread-making, fermentation and wild food foraging.

395 Mentmore Terrace, E8 3PH; e5bakehouse.com

⑱ Hill & Szrok
Modern master butchers

'Small herd, whole carcass' is the description best fitting this meat emporium. By day they sell fine cuts and offal from the finest British livestock. By night the shop transforms into a neighbourhood restaurant. Expect artfully prepared Modern European sharing plates, paired with low-intervention wines and served around a sleek, marble, communal table. Menus change daily based on seasonality, but you can always expect to find a serious steak or two. They also host Rainbow Rooms, a regular pop-up put on by the best chefs in the borough, offering quirky cooking that's kinder to your wallet.

60 Broadway Market, E8 4QJ; hillandszrok.com

Hackney - Eat & Drink

⑲ Koya Ko Hackney
Minimalist Japanese canteen

This low-key Japanese canteen on a corner of Broadway Market only serves variations of two dishes: udon – thick wheat noodles, usually served in broth; and donburi – rice bowls. But this focus is by no means a limiting factor. Classics like udon with prawn tempura and curry rice are expertly and quickly executed. And their karaage (fried chicken) will leave you wishing it was a bottomless bucket. Traditional Japanese breakfasts, as well as English breakfast inspired Japanese dishes, and ice cream sandos, green teas and Japanese beers, mean you can have all kinds of dining experiences here. Koya Ko have sites in Soho and the City, but the Broadway branch benefits from some al fresco seating.
10-12 Broadway Market Mews, E8 4TS;
koya.co.uk

⑳ OMBRA
Venice on Vyner Street

An Italian for Italians and for Brits wanting to bring back memories of their holidays. The pitch is plain. Homemade pasta, seasonal antipasti, low-intervention wines and spritzes, inside an unpretentiously modern dining room, with a terrace overlooking Regents' Canal. The restaurant doubles as a chic brunch destination during weekdays. Menus rotate daily and dining pop-ups happen semi-regularly. Keep an eye on social media to find out about up and coming culinary events.
1 Vyner Street, E2 9DG
ombrabar.restaurant

㉑ pockets
London's best falafel

London isn't known for its falafel, but one plant-based pita place by London Fields is changing all that. Pockets are unorthodox. Fried potato cake and pickled mango might make a traditionalist mad, but it pays off, because this is without question the best falafel you can get in the city. The result of doing only one thing but doing it just right. Their pillowy pita is so perfect it should be patented. Somehow, it doesn't get soggy despite the volume of sauce and stretches to accommodate enough filling to leave you satisfied. At around £9 a serving, pockets are not cheap but the queues here are a testament to the fact that people will pay a little more for the best.
367 Mentmore Terrace, E8 3RT

㉒ Victoria Park Market
Park it at the market

A little sister to Columbia Road and Broadway, Victoria Park Market is a fine alternative to busier weekend affairs. Mingle amongst locals, peruse fresh organic produce and fill up on grub from both emerging & established street food suppliers. Sri Lankan kotthus emit irresistible aromas, fried chicken sizzles on the griddles and fluorescent, freakish pastries swivel heads. Its a great little market to visit for street food and groceries and Victoria Park is the perfect place to enjoy an alfresco lunch.
55-57 Gore Road, E9 7HN;
victoriaparkmarket.com

Hackney - Eat & Drink

Outdoors

㉓ London Fields
Hackney's busiest green space

On fine days, time spent relaxing in London Fields makes for a defining day out in the capital. The drifting smoke from disposable barbecues (now prohibited), the clinking of beer bottles and the buzz of joyful chatter is familiar to many from far and wide, and if it isn't to you, we suggest you make it a priority. For starters, Broadway Market lies just metres away to the south, so you're never far from raucous pubs, great restaurants and independent shops. However, this Green Flag green space has a lot to offer. The two large and well-equipped playgrounds are easily monitored from picnic spots and there are free public toilets. The sports facilities include the renowned 50m heated lido with café (see p.124), cricket pitch, BMX track, outdoor gym, tennis courts and table-tennis tables. It's hard to ignore quite how vital this verdant public park is to locals and life in the surrounding area. A day out here is likely to leave you cherishing it as they do.

London Fields, E8 3EU

㉔ Regents Canal
The most tranquil way to explore Hackney

Regents Canal was built in the early 19th century by John Nash, the architect behind Regency icons like Buckingham Palace, and named after the Prince Regent (later George IV). The canal was originally commercial and accommodated barges transporting cargo to and from The Thames. Today, this industrial past has been mostly subsumed by the flow of people, who enjoy it as an ideal route for pleasure cruising on narrowboats, their cycle commute, or as pedestrians popping between Broadway Market and Victoria Park. Its full extent runs for just over eight and a half miles between Limehouse and Paddington, with popular westerly attractions like Little Venice, Regents Park and King's Cross along the way. But the eastern stretch between Bonner Gate (from where you'll get the most picturesque view), and the unmissable Sharks! installation near Haggerston, with the Bethnal Green Gasholders in between, provides more than enough to feast your eyes upon. Should you want more of the same quaintly urban vibe, a good option is to take the connecting Hertford Union Canal. This takes you alongside the eastern edge of Victoria Park and into Hackney Wick where you'll find many canalside cafés and bars.

25 Victoria Park
Be picky, choose Vicky

Known historically as 'The People's Park' but fondly as 'Vicky' by locals, this is an entirely different beast to London Fields and Hackney's other bijou green spaces. Covering 213 acres, it's an expanse large enough to get lost in, not least because there are endless things to enjoy here. The park has won numerous Green Flag awards and is a great place to just relax without a plan and enjoy the pretty views of the lake, pagoda, three cafés, playgrounds and ornamental gardens, all of which will keep you amused on fine days.

However, should you be the sporty type, there's free & open cricket nets and pitches, a skate park, several football fields, a bowling green, four tennis courts, and an excellent outdoor gym close to a slightly ragged but still usable 400 metre track. Pedalos are a romantic re-addition to activities on the lake and close-by is The Pavilion Café and at the other end of the park The Hub Café. Vicky draws in millions annually, and with its weekend market (see p.134) and incredible facilities, it's one of the things that makes this neighbourhood a great place to spend a day.

Grove Road, E3 5TB

Hackney - Outdoors

Shoreditch

Shoreditch has several potential origin stories, but its name likely comes from being close to one of the city's many ditches. St. Leonard's church was founded in Saxon times, and some of the first performances of Shakespeare's plays took place around here. The neighbourhood has been a hub of industry and haven for Huguenot, Jewish and Bengali refugees and migrants for centuries, but since the 1990s has become one of London's most fashionable areas. Gentrification has seen the arrival of tech companies, vintage markets and vinyl outlets, as well as smart cafés and luxury restaurants – all flourishing side by side with the remnants of the local working-class past. This mix of old and new makes Shoreditch one of the best neighbourhoods in London for a day out. On Sundays, Columbia Road Flower Market is the perfect starting point for your itinerary, especially as it's only a short walk away from Brick Lane and Broadway Market (see page 128). Brick Lane is busy throughout the week as a popular place for both vintage shopping and Bangladeshi restaurants, while also being home to the world-famous Beigel Bake, where you'll find the best beigels in London that are always worth queuing for. After a day exploring the streets and shops on foot, it's worth bunkering down at one of the many swanky eateries or lively pubs for an evening of hedonism. But if you prefer to learn about the local heritage, seek out Dennis Severs' House or the Museum of the Home to find out more about Shoreditch's past.

SHOREDITCH

1. Brick Lane Market
2. Columbia Road Flower Market
3. Spitalfields Market
4. Dennis Severs' House
5. Museum of the Home
6. Rich Mix
7. Goodhood
8. Labour and Wait
9. Libreria Bookshop
10. Rough Trade East
11. SCP
12. Two Columbia Road
13. Beigel Bake
14. Brat
15. Brawn
16. The Cocktail Trading Co.
17. The Golden Heart
18. Leila's
19. Marksman Public House
20. Rochelle Canteen
21. Arnold Circus
22. Hackney City Farm

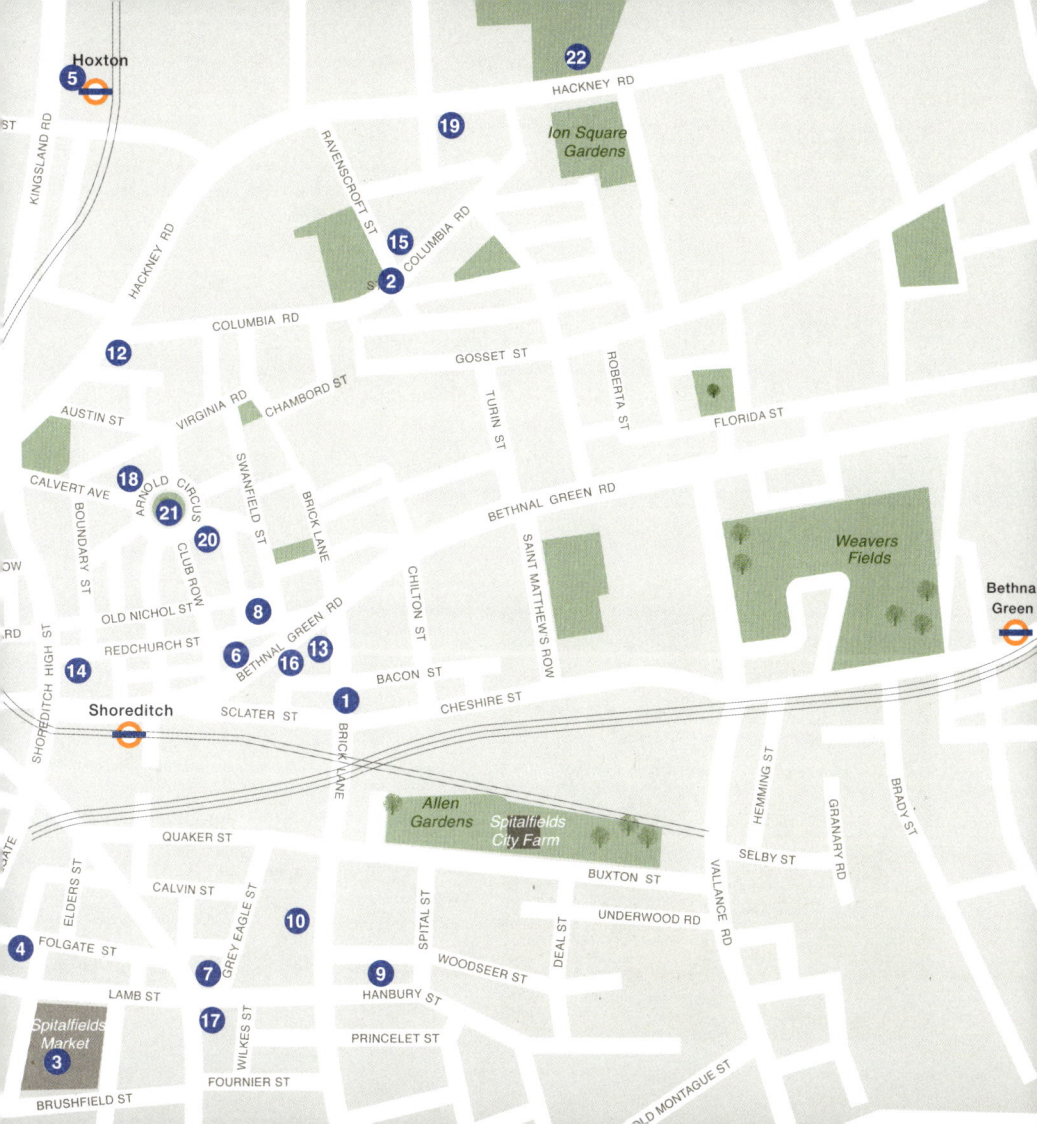

Visit

❶ Brick Lane Market
East London's historic heart

While some of the old chaos of Brick Lane market has been lost to gentrification, it remains the epicentre of East London. Distinct from other markets in the area, not least for its disjointed layout, it runs from Bethnal Green Road to Hanbury Street and is home to, amongst other things, the highest concentration of Bangladeshi restaurants in the city. The area surrounding Truman Brewery has become the heart of a trendy shopping complex, housing various indoor spaces that provide a platform for small businesses. In recent years, the market has expanded with the addition of the bustling subterranean Vintage Market and a smaller retail area known as The Tea Rooms and Rinse Showroom.

At the Bethnal Green end of the market, visitors can explore everything from fruit & veg and bric-à-brac traders to designer boutiques and the internationally famous Beigel Bake. For a taste of old Shoreditch, head down to Sclater Street on a Sunday, where ramshackle stalls in the courtyard still exude the spirit of the past. The chess man, who plays with members of the public for fun, adds to the unique atmosphere. Follow the music, and you'll discover the Backyard Market, a large concrete warehouse with numerous stalls selling designer goods. Additionally, The Upmarket is a spacious venue with boutique shopping avenues and cafés, along with well over a hundred street food stalls.

Shops like ATIKA, Levison's Vintage Clothing and 194 Local ensure the area remains ever-popular with young people, while Brick Lane Bikes and Brick Lane Bookshop continue to service locals. Check out Dark Sugars for the most indulgent hot chocolate you've ever tasted, or else the London Tea Exchange if you're less of a sweet tooth. Flashback Records and Rough Trade East provide for vinyl lovers, and the Pride of Spitalfields – next door to the Gilbert & George centre – is a refreshingly old-school pub that's perfect for a post-market pint.
Brick Lane, E1 6SB;
vintage-market.co.uk; sundayupmarket.co.uk

Shoreditch - Visit

❷ Columbia Road Flower Market
East London's ultimate Sunday ritual
Columbia Road Flower Market is easy to find – just follow the opposite direction of Londoners laden with plants. But it attracts more than gardening enthusiasts, with its gift shops, eateries, and two courtyards offering new and vintage goods. Even on rainy days, buskers provide a musical backdrop on the corner of Ezra Street. The market's stock varies with the seasons, featuring bedding plants in spring, evergreens in autumn, and herbs year round. During the festive season, Columbia Road is the ideal place to find Christmas trees and other yuletide greenery. Some market shops open in the evenings before Christmas for gift shopping, mulled wine, and carols too.

The market gets crowded, with people carrying armfuls of plants resembling *The Day of the Triffids*, but one can escape the throng by exploring the shops lining the street. Here, you can find anything from gifts, furniture, toys, and hats with Harry Brand at no. 122 and Epitome at no.136 firm favourites. Ezra Street and its adjoining courtyards, should not be missed, where you'll find the bearded Shaun selling bric-à-brac as he has for years. Columbia Road is within walking distance of so many other attractions in the area. While a cupful of fried calamari from Lee's Sea Food will keep you going, there's nowhere better to book a Sunday Roast in London than The Marksman, whose pies, beef buns and brown butter tart are the stuff of culinary legend.
Columbia Road, E2 7RG; columbiaroad.info

❸ Spitalfields Market
Shopping centre with a market at its centre
This vast Victorian building once housed a wholesale fruit and veg market but has now been transformed into a smart shopping complex with a vibrant market at its centre. At the commercial Road end is the original building where there are food stalls offering dishes from around the world and where the collectors and vintage stalls are to be found. Further back the environment becomes more contemporary with glass office blocks above and large brands like Lululemon and Amazon cosmetics occupying the smart shops. It's in this smart environment that the craft and fashion stalls are to the fore offering quality textiles, jewellery and gifts. The area has lost a good deal of it's down at heal charm, but the place is always busy and the market now trades throughout the week with the vintage and collectables market on Thursdays always worth a visit.
Brushfield Street, E1 6AA;
spitalfields.co.uk

❹ Dennis Severs' House
A dreamlike historic house

Dennis Severs' House is truly unique – neither museum nor historic house, it's best approached as an art installation. The 18th-century terraced dwelling is designed as a series of atmospheric period vignettes. Severs (who died in 1999) had strong views about how it should be experienced – visitors are expected to be seen and not heard, and a museum-worthy rule of looking but not touching is enforced. In the past Severs would eject visitors who transgressed.

The conceit is that the house is still lived in by a family of Huguenot silk weavers, and going around you'll repeatedly enter rooms they have supposedly just left. Subtle sounds and authentic touches such as brimming bedside chamber pots, unmade beds and food being prepared in the kitchen, help to create the Marie Celeste effect. However, the house remains an engagingly leaky time capsule. Period pedants may disapprove but playful anachronisms abound, including poignant reminders of Severs' own occupancy – a NY Yankees baseball jacket draped over the back of a chair, a pair of highly polished English gent's shoes tucked away in a bedroom. The house evokes several time periods, following successive generations of the Jervis family on a picturesque journey from genteel Hanoverian prosperity to the Dickensian hard times evoked by the squalid top-floor garret. Special champagne evenings, held on the last Thursday of the month, offer a more intimate opportunity to explore the house.

18 Folgate Street, E1 6BX;
dennissevershouse.co.uk

❺ Museum of the Home
The history of English domestic life

Set in 18th-century almshouses, the Museum of the Home is one of London's most charismatic museums. Visitors get the chance to observe the changing face of English middle-class interior decoration. A walk through the original buildings takes visitors from the oak-panelled simplicity of the 17th-century hall to the coolly elegant Georgian parlour and onto a cluttered Victorian sitting room. Another display explores how modern homes are made, ideas of entertainment in the home and how immigrant communities have made British homes their own. In addition to the permanent collection is a lively programme of exhibitions. In December the period rooms are decorated in appropriately festive fig, while in the summer the beautiful walled herb garden is the main attraction. Regardless of the season, the café and museum shop are also well worth a visit.

136 Kingsland Road, E2 8EA;
museumofthehome.org.uk

❻ Rich Mix
Iconic community arts hub

Rich Mix is a charity-run cinema and cross-arts centre, set in a converted leather factory. It offers free arts and culture events over five floors and features three screens showcasing both mainstream and independent films. It also provides flexible performance spaces for thousands of emerging and established artists to rehearse and showcase their work.

35-47 Bethnal Green Rd, E1 6LA; richmix.org.uk

Shoreditch - Visit

Shoreditch - Shop

Shop

❼ Goodhood
Go-to shopping spot for East End hipsters
A hangout spot for London's hipsters, Goodhood has for many years been a premier streetwear store. They stock both emergent and established names in womenswear, menswear, cosmetics, household products and high-end outdoor gear. This is where to discover independent Japanese labels and European brands that set the trends. Although much of the stock is upmarket, you can still bag some affordable gifts like t-shirts, perfume, hats and trinkets.

15 Hanbury Street, E1 6QR;
goodhoodstores.com

❽ Labour and Wait
Utilitarian emporium
This green-tiled household goods shop is a local favourite. Housed in a former pub, they're the pre-eminent purveyors of classic British, European and Japanese products. Whether you're after kitchenware like enamel pots and cups, brushes for every type of cleaning, workwear like Breton shirts, or else the perfect Swiss army knife – every base is covered. The shop is a lesson in timeless design, with a lot of the long-standing brands that even your grandmother would recognise. You can rest assured the hardware you buy here will last you a lifetime, and you can also source everyday items like twine, soap and shoe polish.

85 Redchurch St, E2 7DJ; labourandwait.co.uk

9 Libreria Bookshop
An antidote to Amazon.com
Libreria is one of London's most beautiful bookshops. Inspired by Borges' short story *The Library of Babel*, it aims to cure information overload by tailoring their stock and arranging it not according to standard categories, but in suggestive themes designed to aid browsers. Examples include 'Wanderlust', 'Utopia' and 'The City' with the spotlight on cutting-edge independent publishers. It's also a digital-free zone – all intended as an antidote to Amazon. Do look out for their occasional extremely late-night opening, events that range beyond the standard author Q&A, and a printing press in the basement.

65 Hanbury Street, E1 5JL; libreria.io

10 Rough Trade East
East London's LP emporium
Rough Trade East has been the best place to buy vinyl in Shoreditch for almost two decades. One of the biggest record shops in London, it was designed by starchitect Sir David Adjaye in the Old Truman Brewery, and doubles as a cavernous events space too, with bands and artists regularly playing live. Alongside vinyl, you'll find merchandise like t-shirts and posters and a large book department. At the front of the store there's also a great café to relax and admire your latest purchases.

Old Truman Brewery, 91 Brick Lane, E1 6QL; roughtrade.com

Shoreditch - Shop

⓫ SCP
Multi-floored furniture Mecca
In 1985, Sheridan Coakley founded SCP in a historic London factory building. They debuted with a furniture exhibition featuring Philippe Starck's designs from Café Costes in Paris and a logo, invitation and catalogue by Peter Saville. No longer happy to reproduce designs, Coakley sought out young designers like Jasper Morrison, cementing their position as a pioneering force with their later creation of the Balzac armchair by Matthew Hilton. Today, you'll find in-house designs made in their Norfolk factory, side-by-side with pieces by designers from the global Modernist canon, and some vintage items too. Although out-of-budget for many, an exploration of their towering showroom never fails to inspire.
135-139 Curtain Road, EC2A 3BX; scp.co.uk

⓬ Two Columbia Road
Small but mighty mid-century showroom
Since 1995 Two Columbia Road has been London's go-to for vintage (mid-century) Scandinavian, European, and North American collectable furniture in exquisite condition. Expect all the big names: Charles and Ray Eames, Ettore Sottsass, Alvar Aalto, Arne Jacobsen and Le Corbusier. They double as a gallery with art by the likes of Sarah Lucas and Wolfgang Tillmans. Whether sourcing individual items or creating entire room settings, they provide comprehensive assistance and impartial long-term advice to clients building their collections.
2 Columbia Rd, E2 7NN; twocolumbiaroad.co.uk

Shoreditch - Eat & Drink

Eat & Drink

⓭ Beigel Bake
24-hour Jewish bakery famous for sensational salt beef beigels

Although Brick Lane is home to two equally well-known beigel shops – not least because they're next-door neighbours – it's the one with the white, red and blue shopfront that has always been this author's favourite. The yellow-fronted competition can claim to have pioneered the rainbow beigel, but when it comes to ridiculously fresh, tasty and generous portions of salt beef or smoked salmon stuffed between two pillowy, boiled-then-baked buns, Beigel Bake is the clear winner. Open since 1974, they sell several thousand beigels every day, owing to the fact there is a (fast-moving) queue throughout the day and this place never shuts. The service is infamously brisk, but when they've kept prices down to as little as a couple of quid for a heartily stuffed sandwich, it would feel wrong if it were any other way. It goes without saying that the salt beef is recommended, best enjoyed with mustard and pickle, and perhaps washed down with a cup of tea and a slice of cheesecake. You can't leave London without having tried one.

159 Brick Lane, E1 6SB

⑭ Brat
Cornwall by way of the Basque country

The name of this restaurant is a Cornish slang term still used by fishermen to mean turbot – the fish that many now make a pilgrimage to this Shoreditch establishment for. Here, they'll find it done in a Basque barbecue style, where the coal creates a temperature low enough that the rendering fat cooks the flesh, producing what is now one of the most acclaimed dishes in London. This is also where you'll find the city's best version of another Basque dish that is the opposite of gently-barbecued fish; that is, San Sebastian cheesecake, burnt so that the exterior is approaching blackened, but with a gooey interior cut through perfectly by the accompanying baked fruit or a glass of sherry. Between turbot and dessert are all manner of other stand-out dishes: the anchovy toast, velvet crab soup or just about any cut of meat, fish or veg that can be cooked over an open flame. Their low-intervention wine list is equally extensive and appealing, whilst the dining room is the essence of casual elegance. Booking a table here might be an extravagance, but it's one you'll remember.

4 Redchurch Street, E1 6JL
bratrestaurant.co.uk

⑮ Brawn
East London's nicest neighbourhood eatery
If St. John is the king of East London restaurants, then Brawn is the prince and heir to the throne. Those in the know will notice their pig wine bottle logo is a nod to the signature of their friends in Smithfield. Even though the menu is Modern European rather than British, there's more than a little that is reminiscent of the styles of cooking and hospitality – Brawn after all is 'head cheese', a cold cut of terrine made from pig or calf's brain in aspic. But there's no reason to fear the menu, for they've built their reputation on the city's best fresh pasta and one of the most extensive natural wine cellars anywhere. Housed inside an old workshop, it's an unpretentiously luxurious experience eating here, with the sometimes-mismatched chairs and tables, chalkboards and workwear-clad waiters. For the ultimate family lunch or date night dinner, book a table at Brawn, and don't forget to order their dreamy panna cotta.
49 Columbia Road, E2 7RG; brawn.co

⑯ The Cocktail Trading Co.
High-concept cocktails
Situated at the top of Brick Lane, Cocktail Trading Co. is everything you'd want from a cocktail bar, with a twist. You'll find live music and a dimly lit, plushly decorated bar with bottle green booths, caricatures on the walls and tankards full of monkey nuts. The bar itself looks a lot like a library, with a kaleidoscopic array of bottles. But when you order a cocktail, you'll likely be in for a whimsical surprise. The imaginative drinks on offer here are often served up in surprising styles, such as in a safe, Fabergé egg or with a pair of edible (white chocolate) dentures inside. Of course, you can also order off-menu classics with every drink costing £12, which will feel eminently reasonable once you see the expert preparation of these drinks.
68 Bethnal Green Road, E1 6GQ; thecocktailtradingco.com

⑰ The Golden Heart
The queen of Shoreditch pubs
Shoreditch is home to more pubs per square metre than almost anywhere else in London, and many deserve a mention. But in the 40-odd years that Sandra Esquilant has been the landlady of The Golden Heart, it has truly had a special place in the heart of so many people. It has traded opposite Spitalfields market since the 1900s when the Truman Brewery stood tall in the area (and still does with the neon signage above the pub). Today it is known for its famous clientele, particularly the YBAs in the 90s. Regardless, it's simply a great place for a pint of Guinness in a proper setting with a wrap-around wooden bar and an ever-present throng of punters. To top it all off, you can enjoy some internationally-acclaimed fish & chips from Poppies next door for the way home.
110 Commercial Street, E1 6LZ

Shoreditch - Eat & Drink

Shoreditch - Eat & Drink

⑱ Leila's
The deli of your dreams
This charming organic grocer and café straddles two units on Calvert Avenue, the picturesque street that takes you from the bustle of Shoreditch High Street onto the bucolic Boundary Estate. The café is just as much of an urban oasis as its neighbour, thanks to owner Leila McAlister's masterful appreciation of seasonal produce. Both the café and shop feature minimalist wooden furniture by long-time collaborator Michael Marriott. Eating and shopping under the awnings of this unique deli is one of the most satisfying experiences Shoreditch has to offer.

15-17 Calvert Avenue, E2 7JP; leilasshop.co.uk

⑲ Marksman Public House
The pub that always hits the spot
The Marksman has been in business for over 150 years, but the bygone denizens of this boozer could hardly have imagined it now. Chef-owners Jon Rotheram and Tom Harris transformed it into the gastropub of East London. A Sunday Roast institution, their signature buns and slices of brown butter tart are all firm favourites. Jon and Tom are alumni of St JOHN, so always look out for their pies. Spread across a traditional downstairs pub, a modern upstairs dining room and a roof terrace, you can experience what a pub ought to be. Regardless of whether you stop by for a pint or book a three course meal, any day out in Shoreditch should end up here.

254 Hackney Rd, E2 7SB;
marksmanpublichouse.com

⑳ Rochelle Canteen
A lesson in European cooking in an old East London school
Rochelle Canteen is still very much its own school of cooking. The brainchild of Margot Henderson, it wears the nose-to-tail ethos lightly, meaning they experiment with non-British and non-offal ingredients and recipes without losing sight of the locality and seasonality that makes their menu so special. Found within an old school building, you enter via an exquisite garden (after finding the door – press the 'canteen' buzzer), which is the perfect primer for an afternoon or evening of good eating. Whether you dine inside or out, expect familiar dishes executed to perfection. Special mention goes to the dinner events they regularly organise, which you can stay plugged into via their email newsletter.

16 Playground Gardens, E2 7FA;
rochellecanteen.com

Outdoors

㉑ Arnold Circus
Oasis in London's oldest estate
Forming the centre of London's first ever council estate, this Grade-II listed bandstand and garden helped transform a former slum into a beautiful red brick housing complex that is rightly regarded as a highpoint of the Arts and Crafts movement. However, architect Owen Fleming may not have foreseen back in 1890 how the space would today bring together local artists and the Bangladeshi community to create one of the most desirable buildings to live in. Thanks to the Friends of Arnold Circus, the space has been preserved as an urban oasis that feels miles away from the bustle of nearby Shoreditch High Street. Perfect for enjoying some peaceful contemplation, or perhaps reading a book, don't forget to check out the surrounding attractions like Rochelle Canteen and Leila's café.
Arnold Circus, E2 7JS

㉒ Hackney City Farm
A taste of farm life in the heart of Hackney
This little oasis just off Hackney Road and within a few minutes of Columbia Road, is well worth a visit for a chance to check out some farm animals, enjoy their little garden and do a little shopping at the farm shop. The farm is free to enjoy and offers courses in practical things like bike maintenance and pottery. If making some fury friends gives you an appetite, the farm has the wonderful Frizzante Café on hand offering delicious Italian cuisine and great coffee.
1a Goldsmiths Row, E2 8QA;
hackneycityfarm.co,uk

Shoreditch - Outdoors

Walthamstow

Walthamstow was a rural village until the 19th century, when local innovations in transport helped transform it into a London suburb. It's still very much a peripheral part of the capital, but having a day out here is essential for anyone looking to explore a different side of city life. Walthamstow Market might be the longest in the country, and is one of the few surviving street markets where you can find just about anything. The neighbourhood also has some major cultural highlights, including the William Morris Gallery, the former home of the father of the Arts & Crafts Movement, which is now dedicated to his life and work. For those looking to soak in some of the area's industrial past in the present, head to Blackhorse Road, which has factory outlets and independent breweries. After visiting a local taproom, head to God's Own Junkyard, an Aladdin's cave of neon signage. But best of all are Walthamstow's many green spaces, including Epping Forest – the largest in London – as well as the genteel Lloyd Park, and the wilder Walthamstow Wetlands.

Visit

❶ God's Own Junkyard
The most lit-up place in London
Probably the most photogenic industrial lot in the world, God's Own Junkyard is the brainchild of the late neon-sign maker Chris Bracey, who started out designing the pieces that lit up Soho's strip clubs and brothels, before transitioning to custom work for films. His clients have included Stanley Kubrick, Tim Burton and Christopher Nolan. Now, his old workshop and storage space functions as a shop and photoshoot spot. It's a great place to enjoy the ambience and one of the best light shows in London, but if you've got deep pockets, you can also buy a sign.

Unit 12, Ravenswood Industrial Est, Shernhall Street, E17 9HQ; godsownjunkyard.co.uk

❷ Ravenswood Industrial Estate
Micro industrial estate for micro breweries
This rather functional industrial estate is not only the home of God's Own Junkyard, but also boasts three micro-breweries and a gin distillery – all of whom sell their delicious intoxicating liquor in their taprooms or to enjoy at home. Wildcard Brewery and Real Al Taproom are among the businesses to also offer great food to help absorb all the alcohol and there are occasional pop-up caterers at the weekend. Take a look at their website to find out more.

Shernhall St, E17 9HQ; ravenswoodcollective.com

❸ Red Imp Comedy Club
Warm-up spot for stars of stand-up
Red Imp is a place for recognisable names in comedy to practice their performances before TV, as well as emergent talent to try their luck. The Comedy Club is East London's best destination for stand-up nights. Upstairs at Ye Olde Rose and Crown, it usually runs the first Wednesday or Thursday of the month. Past acts include Micky Flanagan, Omid Djalili and Alan Carr.

Ye Olde Rose & Crown Theatre,
55 Hoe Street, E17 4SA;
redimpcomedy.com

❹ Soho Theatre – Walthamstow
West End meets the East End
The old cinema on Hoe Street was a throwback to the golden age of film. Built in the 1930s in a striking Art Deco style, it once seated over 2,000 people. Known as The Granada, it experienced a gradual decline before finally closing its doors in 2003. Shortly after, a campaign started to save the building and restore it as a cultural landmark. In 2025, the beautifully renovated venue reopened as the East London branch of Soho Theatre on Dean Street. Today, it hosts a vibrant arts programme, with comedy taking centre stage. Performers such as Dara Ó Briain, Phil Wang, and Tim Minchin have brought their talents to E17, once again transforming the venue into a thriving cultural hub at the heart of Walthamstow.

186 Hoe Street, E17 4QH;
sohotheatre.com

Walthamstow - Visit

❺ Walthamstow Village
The historic centre of the borough
The oldest part of Walthamstow and a designated conservation area, the Village centres on the 12th-century St. Mary's Church and the surrounding streets, that are also home to historic buildings. Most notable of these is the 15th-century timber-framed hall house called The Ancient House. Along the same street are the Monoux Almshouses, which are Grade-II listed. They were founded in 1527 to provide shelter for the elderly and continue to do so today. If you want to learn more about the area, head to the nearby Vestry House Museum, which has previously been used as a workhouse and police station. Since 1931 it has held the archives of the borough, exhibiting local history and also running the local studies library.

Orford Road, the ancient road leading up to St Mary's Church, has in recent years developed as a street of quaint restaurants, cafés, pubs and shops. eat17 is one of the most well-known – an award-winning grocer, trading there since 2006. Froth & Rind is the best place to source artisanal cheese, while Finamore can satisfy all your antique needs.

28-30 Orford Road, E17 9NJ

❻ William Morris Gallery
Museum dedicated to the founder of the Arts & Crafts movement
This award-winning museum celebrates William Morris, the founding father of the Arts and Crafts movement. A powerhouse of energy and creativity, Morris was also an entrepreneur, poet, translator, Socialist, typographer, and pioneering conservationist. No wonder the cause of his death (in 1896) was given as 'being William Morris and having done more work than most men'. Morris lived in this grand Georgian house from his teens to his early twenties and it has been a gallery devoted to him since 1950. The gallery captures the essence of the man with just the right blend of scholarship and affection. A series of beautifully re-displayed galleries guide visitors through Morris's extraordinary life, from nature-loving childhood and student days at Oxford, to his friendship with the Pre-Raphaelite artists, his enduring legacy as a designer, and his later career as a typographer and publisher. Exhibits range from stained glass panels to sturdy rustic furniture and Morris' signature nature-themed textiles and wallpapers. Displays reveal some of the luxury commissions that helped make Morris & Co a household name, while 'The Workshop' looks at the labour-intensive craft techniques behind the tapestries, furniture and fabrics that Morris designed. If you show up on Saturday, keep an eye peeled for the Lloyd Park Market within the grounds of the gallery (see p.177).

Lloyd Park, Forest Road, E17 4PP;
wmgallery.org.uk

Shop

❼ Blackhorse Lane Atelier
London's only craft jeans manufacturer

Opened in 2016, Blackhorse Lane Ateliers was founded by Bilgehan Ates after 25 years in the industry. The workshop is open to visitors, so you can see how their jeans are made before browsing the finished products. Each pair of jeans are produced under the roof of this restored 1920s factory building, using old denim mill machinery from decommissioned Levi's factories and the USSR. There are four models, each named after a London postcode, and a lifetime repair policy for customers.

114b Blackhorse Lane, E17 6AA;
blackhorselane.com

❽ Ebtd
Postmodern furniture paradise

Everything but the Dog (ebtd) has specialised in original modernist and postmodern furniture since 2015. Known for stocking mid-century modern wares in their showroom, they now also offer late 20th century designs, with things like Memphis Design regularly cropping up. Expect to find the biggest names in Italian furniture, such as Kartell, Cassina and B&B Italia, or else pieces by pioneering designers like Vico Magistretti, Mario Bellini and Anna Castelli Ferrieri. Their goods are perfect for the aspiring maximalist – colourful cloud chairs, marble coffee tables and funkily-shaped lamps.

Rear of 70 Hoe Street, E17 4PG; ebtd.co.uk

❾ The Every Space
Independent plant & gift shop

Founded by interior designer Caroline Johnston, this independent business has grown from a market stall to two shops in just five years, a mark of its proprietor's considerable talent for curating beautiful products. Part-gift shop, part-plant shop, the former is a minimal space brought to life by a colourful array of homewares, women's accessories, beauty products, books and stationery. The latter is a living jungle of houseplants, pots and flowers. Caroline also regularly runs workshops on plant care and indoor gardening, such as terrarium making, so it's a great way of getting involved in the community.

5 & 6 Central Parade, 137 Hoe Street, E17 4RT;
theeveryspace.com

❿ Krypton Komics
Neighbourhood comic store

Krypton is a heavyweight amongst comic book stores, with over 35 years in the business. They stock a colossal range of American comics from 1945 to the present, with over 10,000 titles available and more than a quarter of a million listed on the website, with prices from £2 upwards. Most important of all, this is a back-issue haven, where the serious collector comes with their list to forage through the many boxes of old comics for a missing issue in their collection.

94 Blackhorse Lane, E17 6AA;
kryptoncomicsonline.com

Walthamstow - Shop

⑪ Walthamstow Market
One of London's longest markets

Many locals claim this is Britain's longest market, although Portobello is surely longer. Even so, it's a fair distance from St James Street to the end of the market at Hoe Street. Walthamstow is thiving, in part due to the pedestrianisation of the wide thoroughfare of Walthamstow High Street, making it a great place for shopping and strolling. The adjacent shops also complement the market, with some excellent butchers, fishmongers and international food retailers. There are about 300 stalls lining the half-mile strip, selling anything from groceries to kitchenware and kids' toys. The clothing isn't as trendy as that at markets like Camden, but there are high street fashion bargains to be found at those selling overstocks and slight seconds from big name brands. If you are more interested in making your own clothes or curtains, there are several fabric sellers too. The usual fresh fruit and veg stalls compete for your business with generously discounted bulk offers, and with fishmongers and butchers beside them, you can do your entire weekly shop here. If you want something to eat while on the go, the many street food stalls have you covered, and First Stop Café is a great caff. Saturdays are the best day to visit and on Sundays the market gives way to a smaller farmers' market that occupies the Town Square. It's a great place to source quality fresh veg and meat and has become a firm favourite with locals.
High Street, E17 7JX;
walthamstowsundaysocial.com

⓬ Wood Street Indoor Market
Vintage market in an old cinema

A cinema until 1955, this indoor vintage market underwent a transformation in 2012 and now resembles a circus big top. It's laid out around a horseshoe-shaped corridor, housing 30 distinct units occupied by collectors and antique dealers. The corridors are filled with crates of vinyl records, racks of dazzling cabaret costumes, and scattered enamel pots, creating a labyrinthine space that's easy to get lost in. If vintage goods are your thing, you'll likely end up with a bagful of bric-à-brac for less than a fiver.
98-100 Wood Street, E17 3HX;
woodstreetindoormarket.co.uk

Eat & Drink

⓭ Blackhorse Beer Mile
East End rival to Bermondsey's Beer Mile

The Blackhorse Beer Mile is a route starting from Blackhorse Road station that runs past the borough's highest concentration of craft breweries. An East End rival to Bermondsey's Beer Mile in South London. All the breweries and wineries have taprooms to sample their produce, as well as plenty of indoor and outdoor seating, and plenty of food like sourdough pizza to accompany the booze. The breweries are, in geographical order: The Brewer's Bar at Signature Brew; Pretty Decent Beer; Exale Brewery taproom; The Beerblefish Brewing Company; Renegade Wine; Wild Card Brewery; and most famously Hackney Brewery, which ends the route near Walthamstow Central station.

171 Shernhall Street, E17 9HX
blackhorsebeermile.co.uk

⓮ Bühler + Co.
Walthamstow's favourite veggie café

At the very top of Hoe Street (close to Lloyd Park and the William Morris Gallery) can be found this excellent veggie café. The interior is light-filled and minimalist, but the food packs a punch with French toast a real treat and the veggie fry-up worth going out of your way to enjoy. Bühler + Co might be a little more pricey than your average greasy spoon but the food here is carefully sourced from local suppliers and the quality of everything on offer, from the cakes to the coffee, make this place great value and a real Walthamstow gem.

8 Chingford Road, E17 4PJ;
buhlerandco.com

⓯ Etles
London's first Uyghur restaurant

This mom-and-pop restaurant was the first in London to offer authentic dishes from Xinjiang – the region of China bordering Central Asia. Chef, Mukaddes Yadikar, and her husband Ablikim Rahman are Uyghurs, and opened Etles to celebrate their cuisine, that is little-known in Britain. It features kebabs, naans, and hand-pulled noodles with lots of spice, indicative of how central this region was to the historic trade in spices along the Silk Road. Etles takes its name from Xinjiang's Atlas silks, the zigzag patterned garb chef Mukaddes wears to work. A majority of her customers are Chinese, who make the pilgrimage for the food and ambience. And we see why, for where else in the city will you find a dining room filled with the traditional instruments and fashions of the Eurasian steppe? Try the Da pan ji, a spicy chicken and potato stew served with hand-pulled noodles, as well as the dumplings.

235 Hoe St, E17 9PP;
etleswalthamstow.com

Walthamstow - Eat & Drink

Walthamstow - Eat & Drink

⑯ Lloyd Park Market
Food market by William Morris Gallery
Between 10am and 4pm every Saturday, Lloyd Park is transformed by the arrival of produce and street food stalls. Many are locals involved in social enterprises, so it's good to know the food you buy is supporting the area's community. With the William Morris Gallery and Lloyd Park right nextdoor, you can get your grocery shopping and grab brunch between seeing incredible art exhibitions and enjoying all that the park has to offer.

Forest Road, E17 4PP;
lloydparkmarket.com

⑰ Made in Portugal
Walthamstow's best-kept culinary secret
The epitome of a local gem, Made In Portugal is part Portuguese deli, part family-run café. They have a deserved reputation for their amazing cooked breakfasts at unbeatable prices. Daily specials mean you'll never get bored, especially when things like Portuguese BBQ ribs are on offer, or else they offer an amazing fry-up between 9am and 2pm. A pint of Super Bock lager on draft is as little as £3.50 and homemade pastries like a pastel de nata or a risolle for just a quid or two. Run by husband-and-wife Anita and Luis Pipas, the café serves the community of this quiet neighbourhood, but you'll be made more than welcome.

171 Shernhall Street, E17 9HX;

⑱ Today Bread
Award-winning baked goods in a Grade-II listed building
Nestled inside the Grade-II listed Central Parade building – a late 1950s shopping complex that embodies the 'Festival of Britain' style – is a thriving creative community and the area's best bakery. Organic sourdough and pastries are freshly made, and you can often see them emerge from the oven while sitting in the dining area. Toasties, seasonal soups, wraps and salads are served 7 days a week and the deli provides for all your pantry needs.

6-10 Central Parade, 137 Hoe Street, E17 4RT
todaybread.com

Outdoors

🆉 Epping Forest
London's largest ancient woodland
An ancient woodland like no other in London, Epping Forest covers some 6,000 acres on the western and northern edges of the borough. Worth exploring first is Queen Elizabeth's Hunting Lodge, which was built under the orders of Henry VIII in 1543 and offers a glimpse into the forest's Tudor past. In the area of High Beach stands Holy Innocents Church, with its 128-feet tower and spire. The area was once the home of a 19th-century private asylum, where poet John Clare was once resident. Another poet with links to the area is Alfred Lord Tennyson, who lived in Beech Hill House in the late 1830s. As one of the last surviving areas of the great oak forests that surrounded London until medieval times, Epping Forest is London's largest open space and a dedicated conservation area. Beyond the trees, sporty types will find sixty football pitches, a golf course, three cricket pitches and horses for hire.

visiteppingforest.org

🆇 Lloyd Park
Walthamstow's perfect little park
Just behind the William Morris Gallery, this Victorian park opened in 1900 and was given a much needed make over in 2012. It's not a huge green space compared to the nearby Epping Forest and wetlands, but manages to pack a good deal in with a kid's playground, outdoor table tennis tables (bring your own bats), tennis courts, basketball courts and outdoor gym. If all this activity leaves you peckish, then head to the café within the grounds, or else the William Morris Gallery café, which has outdoor seating that backs directly onto the park. If you visit on a Saturday you can also try the street food from Lloyd Park Market (10am-4pm), which is best enjoyed on one of the benches in the park's elegant rose garden.

Forest Road, N17 4PP;
friendsoflloydpark.org

㉑ Walthamstow Wetlands
East End Eden for emigrating birds

Walthamstow Wetlands is vast. Cared for by the London Wildlife Trust, the nature reserve spans some 520 acres near the historic Essex-Middlesex border on the River Lea. Centred around the reservoirs built here in the 19th century, this urban wetland is one of the largest of its kind in Europe, serving as a vital pathway for migrating, wintering and breeding birds. A Site of Special Scientific Interest, it supports the most notable variety of breeding wetland birds among a network of London's drinking water reservoirs, with large breeding grounds for domestic species like herons and visitors like lapwing, curlew, ruff and oystercatchers. There are also two Victorian industrial structures on site – the Coppermill, which is Grade-II listed and has been there in some capacity since the 14th century, and the Marine Engine House, which is now a visitor centre, café, shop and exhibition space. Beyond the wetlands are the Lee Valley's canals and several walking paths taking you back towards or further away from east London.

2 Forest Road, N17 9NH;
wildlondon.org.uk

South

Borough & Bermonsey
Brixton
Greenwich

Borough & Bermondsey

Borough and Bermondsey make up one of London's oldest suburbs, stretching back to Roman times. Today, the historic features sit in the shade of the ultramodern, with the Shard towering above all else in the city. The area's past reputation for vice is long gone, as bearbaiting, theatres and prostitution, which were once permitted here, have been replaced by far more respectable pleasures (although Shakespeare's Globe remains). The antiques market that starts early on Friday mornings is the perfect place to get a taste of 'old London', and just around the corner is one of the last surviving traditional pie and mash shops in M. Manze. Right by Southwark Cathedral is Borough Market, which was once a rough-and-ready wholesale site, but is now the capital's preeminent foodie destination, with visitors from around the world coming to sample the stalls, source the best ingredients and soak up the unique atmosphere. If you're interested in history, there are two museums worth seeking out: the Old Operating Theatre and the Fashion and Textile Museum, which has a technicolour exterior that pays homage to its founder, Zandra Rhodes. Meanwhile, contemporary art fans should head straight to the White Cube Gallery on Bermondsey Street. Nearby, Bermondsey Beer Mile has all kinds of hedonistic activities on offer. Meanwhile, the food at Maltby Street Market is the David to Borough's Goliath, packing a punch despite its diminutive size. And although this part of town isn't known for open spaces, there are a few pockets of greenery that provide welcome respite from the bustle of Borough and Bermondsey.

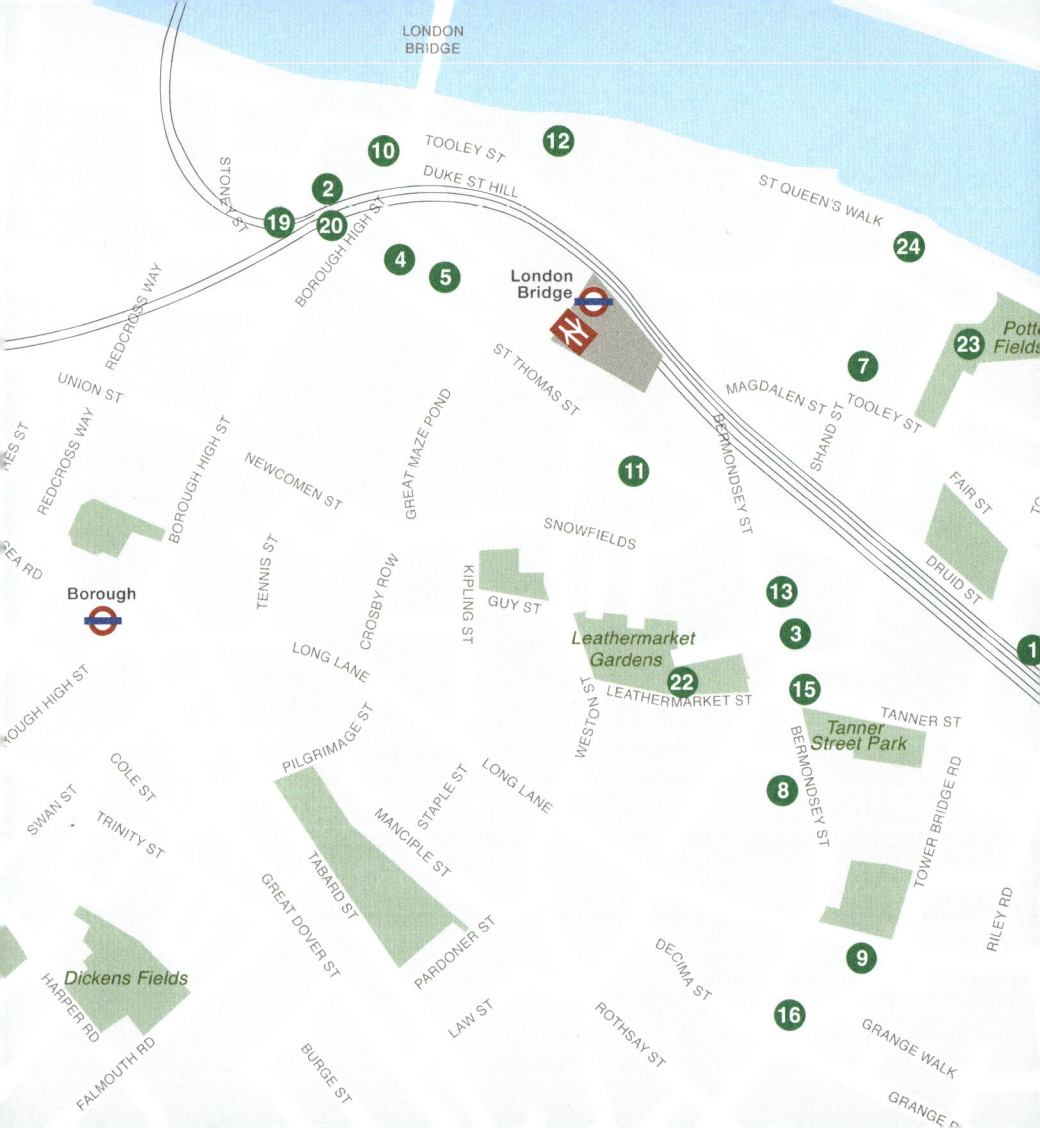

BOROUGH & BERMONDSEY

1. Bermondsey Beer Mile
2. Borough Market
3. Fashion and Textile Museum
4. Old Operating Theatre Museum
5. The Shard
6. Token Studio
7. Unicorn Theatre
8. White Cube Gallery
9. Bermondsey Antique Market
10. Borough Kitchen
11. Flea London Vinegar Yard
12. Hay's Galleria and Riverside Bookshop
13. London Glassblowing
14. Provision
15. Casse-Croute
16. M. Manze
17. Maltby Street Market
18. Magazzino
19. The Market Porter Pub
20. Padella
21. St John Bakery
22. Leathermarket Gardens
23. Potter's Field Park
24. Scoop Amphitheatre

Borough & Bermondsey - Visit

Visit

❶ Bermondsey Beer Mile
Exactly what it says on the bottle

Though the crawl extends to South Bermondsey's Fourpure and Small Beer Brew Co., most bars, breweries and distilleries gather under the arches just a stone's throw from the neighbourhood's centre. Enid Street is a good starting point, close to several establishments, like the craft-scene renegade Cloudwater and table beer titans The Kernel. After sampling any number of experimental ales available here, take a right on Abbey Street before passing the bridge onto Druid Street. This final stretch is home to many more businesses, like Anspach & Hobday, who make 'London Black', a fantastic homage to porter's roots and an antidote to Guinness-fatigue. Many arches also cater to those seeking respite from the boozy bustle that the Beer Mile brings, and you can soak up your drinks from several food spots, including the vendors at Maltby Street Market. If you're a little wobbly after all the alcohol, there are several tube stations within walking distance.
START: 73-75 Enid Street, SE16 3RA;
FINISH: Maltby Street Market, SE1 3PA;
bermondsey-beer-mile.co.uk

❷ Borough Market
London's ultimate foodie market

Visitors to this foodie mecca are likely unaware of quite how much Borough Market has changed in the last 30 years. The wrought iron structure, painted in British Green, tells a story unheard – of a rough and ready wholesale market, working-class to the roots and the sole territory of restaurateurs and traders. Indeed, the market claims to trace itself back to at least 1014, but the market of today is a far more consumer-friendly affair. Visitors here can find the highest quality organic meat from the likes of Rhug Estate Farm, Sea urchins or shellfish from Haward's Oysters and 20 kinds of fungi from Fitz Fine Foods. It is this diversity of produce that has made Borough Market the biggest and best food market in the UK. The street food on offer is a real highlight, and don't miss craft producers and providers like Neal's Yard, Monmouth Coffee and Utobeer. But some things never change. You'll still find Jock Stark, the market's longest-standing trader, selling fruit and veg in the same manner as he has done for the past 50-odd years. The Market Porter pub across the road is as busy as ever. It is this balance of new and old that makes Borough Market a fine example of British food culture.

Southwark Street, SE1 1TL;
boroughmarket.org.uk

❸ Fashion and Textile Museum
Technicolour couture and more

Inspired by the architect's Mexican colour palette and designer-founder Zandra Rhode's psychedelic style, FTM's vibrant yellow and pink façade is impossible to miss. This alone has made it a 'destination', but the rotating exhibition programme is a must-see for fashion enthusiasts. Keeping a strong focus on fashion and style from the post-war period, workshops and master classes offer experimentation with couture. The shop's edit of fashion design books, sewing patterns and accessories, plus a pleasant café, makes this a must-visit for lovers of fashion.

79-85 Bermondsey Street, SE1 3XF;
ftmlondon.org

❹ Old Operating Theatre Museum
A gladiator pit of surgical scars

The Old Operating Theatre Museum's discovery after 100 years in a baroque church attic is a divine intervention against nearby London Dungeons. A rickety bell-ringers' staircase primes the nerves for a macabre wooden arena, baring scars as Europe's oldest operating theatre predating anaesthetics and antiseptic. Surgical saws and human specimens keep the spirit of this grisly educational space alive. The shop's a good browse too, carrying books, rubber organs and much in between.

9a St Thomas Street, SE1 9RY;
oldoperatingtheatre.com

Borough & Bermondsey - Visit

❺ The Shard
Dubai-on-Thames

Fast becoming London's most recognisable landmark, The Shard draws more awe than the capital's other skyscrapers combined. Postmodern architect Renzo Piano's best-known project impales the skyline 70m above Canary Wharf; its peak crowns at 309.6 metres, or 1,016 feet – the highest in Western Europe. Some see it as a welcome addition to the cityscape; others see a 95-storey carbuncle threatening the surrounding historic architecture. It'd be foolhardy to deny though, that on a sunny day the surface's 11,000 glass panes make quite an impression on the visitor. Don't just admire the spectacle from outside – at nearly twice the height of other viewing platforms in London, the 68th, 69th and 72nd floors offer 360-degree views for up to 40 miles, taking in the beauty of London below. There's even the chance to do yoga from this height, or alternatively, experience it all from their 5-star Shangri-La Hotel and several luxury restaurants & bars. Indeed, dining at such opulent heights is on most Londoner's bucket list. Regardless of your feelings toward it, the millions it attracts every year means The Shard will weather time as a stalagmite of London's skyline. Do book in advance to avoid any disappointment.

32 London Bridge Street, SE1 9SG; the-shard.com

⑥ Token Studio
Workshop under the arches
As much of Druid Street is taken up by the breweries of Bermondsey's Beer Mile, this community-focused creative studio is a breath of fresh air. That said, Token are gracious enough to host Bring Your Own Booze pottery events, alongside a wealth of other activities, including painting, candle-making, knitting & crochet, leatherwork, and beauty product creation, using vegan and organic materials. Classes run most days (and nights) of the week, although it's necessary to book in advance to avoid disappointment. A great option for groups, couples, or any one looking to meet new people and get creative in the area. The business is also very family-friendly with lots of workshops for kids. As it's a stone's throw from Bermondsey's other attractions, you can easily fit a session here into your day's itinerary.
76 Druid Street, SE1 2AN; tokenstudio.co.uk

⑦ Unicorn Theatre
Mythical menagerie for London's young talent
Unique to London, this young persons' theatre and education space is as much a family must-visit because of the award-winning building as for the season of shows for under-18s. With more than 70 years experience, Unicorn Theatre manages to produce 20 plays a year, entertaining 90,000+ children, parents and carers. Unicorn runs several outreach programmes, supported by the likes of Judi Dench and Rory Kinnear.
147 Tooley Street, SE1 2HZ;
unicorntheatre.com

⑧ White Cube Gallery
The mothership of modern art
At its inception, this ex-warehouse was the largest commercial gallery in Europe, earmarked by gallerist Jay Jopling as his empire's flagship. The space features three exhibition halls, a 60-seat auditorium for films and lectures plus a shop for esoteric art books. The spectrum of artists exhibited makes White Cube *the* place to see contemporary conceptual art, frequently showing household British names like Damien Hirst, Tracy Emin and Gilbert & George. Free entry, a great pedestrian thoroughfare, and with Bermondsey's scene in orbit – be sure to peg White Cube on any itinerary of the area.
144-152 Bermondsey Street, SE1 3TQ;
whitecube.com

Shop

⑨ Bermondsey Antique Market
A Friday morning institution

London's oldest antiques market has seen it all, from ramshackle roots to its current, modern site. Despite such change, this market is still unique, beginning life on Friday mornings strictly for serious antique trading. As the day wanes, it turns over to tourists, but you'll still be able to find silverware, jewellery, military memorabilia and even some finds from London's Mudlarkers. Bring your haggling hat, as not all prices are marked (or firm). It's a remarkable place and one of the few remaining genuine antique markets in the capital.

11 Bermondsey Square, SE1 3UN;
bermondseysquare.net

⑩ Borough Kitchen
The chosen place for home cooks

For many years Borough Kitchen has been a top London destination for finding all manner of cooking equipment, spawning two further stores in the capital with cooking schools in each. Next door to the Market Hall's glass atrium, the tall and airy shop interior is home to the best pans, knives and specialist tools that'll take your dinner parties and family meals to the next level. And if you need to polish up on your skills, they run classes on everything from knife sharpening to fermentation.

16 Borough High Street, SE1 9QG;
boroughkitchen.com

⑪ Flea London Vinegar Yard
A flashier style of flea

Representing the new wave of vintage fairs, Flea sits amidst the historic charm of South London's brick warehousing, host to stalls selling it all: fashion, antiques, vinyl, books, furniture, cameras… you name it. The central stalls sit adjacent to a communal bench-seating area, while Vinegar Yard's periphery consists of tempting pop-up food vendors – all the ingredients for visit here. But Vinegar Yard isn't just vintage – you'll find craft-makers amidst the fun, offering contemporary art and design at affordable prices.

Vinegar Yard, St Thomas Street, SE1 3QU;
flealondon.com

Borough & Bermondsey - Shop

⓬ Hay's Galleria & Riverside Bookshop
Books by the riverbank

Few places broadcast the capital's maritime heritage as well as Hay's Galleria. Once 'the Larder of London', this Grade-II listed Wharf stored imported goods for over 300 years. Following regeneration, it's now a multi-purpose space for shops, offices, restaurants and public art, including a 60ft kinetic bronze sculpture. Under the vaulted glass ceiling you'll find a number of chain eateries, but Riverside Bookshop is what makes the excursion worth it. Established here for over 25 years, this indie has knowledgeable staff, a trusted 'recommendations table', and a selection of 10,000+ titles.

Riverside Bookshop – Unit 15, Hay's Galleria, 57 Tooley Street, SE1 2QN; theriversideway.com

⓭ London Glassblowing
Where art meets alchemy

Peter Layton's open studio and shop is a great place to see how 'the grandmaster' of British glassmaking creates his beautiful pieces. Decorative glass pieces are curated in front of a volcanic workshop, where you can watch this intricate process. They run exhibitions throughout the year and offer glassblowing experience days for those who want to try their hand. The prices range from £50 for small 'free blown' pieces to bespoke decorative structures running into the thousands.

62-66 Bermondsey Street, SE1 3UD; londonglassblowing.co.uk

⑭ Provision
Homeware store under the arches

Occupying a cavernous railway arch down on Maltby Street, Provision is the perfect place to take a break from the surrounding street food temptations and enjoy some retail therapy. The photogenic interior – think exposed brick walls and rustic wooden furnishing – makes for the ideal backdrop to their stock of carefully-curated ceramics, apparel, furniture, home fragrances and coffee-table books to mull over. It's a great place to come for some design inspiration, especially vis-à-vis flooring (the business offers a bespoke flooring and tiling service), so you're bound to leave laden with ideas. If your budget doesn't quite cover vintage furniture, then there are plenty of smaller things to entice you or make for an inspiring gift. In the wake of the nearby Lassco closing, Provision has stepped in, to become the store of choice for shoppers in Bermondsey.

Arch 53 Ropewalk, Maltby Street, SE1 3PA
Provisionstore.co.uk

Eat & Drink

⓯ Casse-Croûte
More Bordeaux than Bermondsey

At once quirky and classic, Casse-Croûte is a Gallic bistro that combines the quality of haute cuisine with the comfort of a neighbourhood restaurant. Tradition is upheld both in retro décor and a menu featuring duck leg, lapin au vin, pork terrines and mille-feuille. In a similar vein, the wine list, menu and the service are all in French – which explains why Casse-Croûte has become a firm favourite with Bermondsey's Francophiles over the years.

109 Bermondsey Street, SE1 3XB;
cassecroute.co.uk

⓰ M. Manze
Blue plaque pie café

Dating back to 1892, the capital's oldest pie and mash shop, M. Manze, is the place to sample a true local delicacy. Meat pie, mashed potatoes, parsley liquor and jellied eel are historic lunches for hungry Londoners. The essential tiled interiors and marble-tabled booths complement the simplicity of the culinary experience. Don't expect fine dining but do bank on the food being handmade from scratch and the portions generous.

87 Tower Bridge Road, SE1 4TW;
manze.co.uk

⓱ Maltby Street Market
Borough's bijou brother

Though at just a hundred metres long, considerably smaller than neighbouring culinary heavyweight Borough Market, Maltby Street packs an equally heavy gastronomic punch. Hidden down a formerly industrial alley, the crowds are thinner, giving the place far less of a touristy atmosphere, far more a meandering neighbourhood feel. The drinking and dining arrangements are casual – steaming street food stalls line one side; railway arches housing trendy eateries and wine bars on the other. When spoilt with so much choice, it's worth wandering down and back before deciding between tagines, gyozas, London's favourite brownies or the traditional go-to of native oysters with a glass of white wine. The local craft beer scene spills onto the street to collective delight, while the vegan food here is also popular. If you're stretched for time or patience, then 40 Maltby Street, remains one of the market's best spots to eat and drink. It serves the finest of natural Old World wines alongside impeccably sourced and cooked Modern British cuisine. When all this is within a short walk of Bermondsey's other highlights, there aren't many better ways to spend a weekend than at Maltby Street Market.

37 Maltby Street, Rope Walk, SE1 3PA;
maltbystmarket.co.uk

⑱ Magazzino
Beer Mile's wine spot
Having had success with their pizzas a stone's throw away on Maltby Street, the Bon Vino brand have employed their tried-and-tested formula once again, this time under the arches of Bermondsey's Beer Mile on Druid Street. Serving antipasti, Neapolitan pizza and fresh pasta alongside their impressive selection of Italian wines, you can also swing by for simple baked good if you're in a rush. The prices are reasonable, making Magazzino the perfect relaxed alternative to the alcohol fuelled mayhem of the Beer Mile outside.
78 Druid Street, SE1 2AN

⑲ The Market Porter Pub
Best of a dying breed
One of few pubs still trading at 6am, this popular public house is amongst London's most commendable, serving Borough Market's porters side by side with suited gents. Award-winning 'real ales', craft beers and good pub grub, like scotch eggs and pies, keep it full to the rafters most days. The downstairs is a casual affair while, in the upstairs dining room, traditional wooden furnishing retains that Old-World feeling. Choose The Market Porter to see what a proper London pub is all about.
9 Stoney Street, SE1 9AA;
themarketporter.co.uk

⑳ Padella
A pasta lovers' paradise
This modern bistro is one of London's top locations for casual dining. Serving simple yet superb pasta dishes, Padella boasts a Michelin Bib and a notoriously long waiting list, but it's really worth standing in line (or just downloading CleverQueue). With nearly all main dishes under £10, and plenty of affordable starters, desserts and drinks, this cheap eat is great value. Their classic dishes make use of great local ingredients too. An interior to match the food – laid back and attractive – makes Padella as good for solo diners as date nights.
6 Southwark Street, SE1 1TQ; padella.co

㉑ St JOHN Bakery
Pastries and bread under the arches
Fergus Henderson's rule that 'bread is as fundamental on the table as your knife and fork' is one to live by. Here, sourdoughs and custard-filled doughnuts alike, undergo slow fermentation over many hours. Their quality attracts devotees who know you can't find better. We advise you seek out this simple setup under one of Bermondsey's railway arches for unbeatable baked goods from Friday to Sunday. You could also take advantage of their stock of quality wines at shop prices.
72 Druid Street, SE1 2HQ; stjohnrestaurant.com

Outdoors

㉒ Leathermarket Gardens
Pastoral places in urban spaces
Despite the Shard penetrating the skyline, Bermondsey's parks instil somewhat of a village feel, none more so than Leathermarket Gardens. While nearby Tanner Street Park, is functional and equipped with tennis courts, the Gardens are where to unwind, away from the city rush. A stretch of lawn for picnics is only interrupted by rose beds and ornamental trees, so you can share lunchtime with the bumblebees that give this place its buzz.
13 Weston Street, SE1 3HP

㉓ Potter's Field Park
A park with a panorama
With an unrivalled view of Tower Bridge and many other landmarks, this park is one of few along the Thames offering respite from the hustle, bustle and endlessly built-up environment. 50 plant species makeup perennial beds running throughout the park, while there are many types of tree under which lunch from the nearby cafés can be enjoyed. Asides from the pleasant flora and fauna, there are regular events going on, easily discovered via the park's Instagram page.
Tooley Street / Tower Bridge Road, SE1 2AA;
pottersfield.co.uk

㉔ Scoop Amphitheatre
A Midsummer Day's Dream
From June to August, Scoop hosts sports screenings like Wimbledon and London's only annual season of free, professional theatrical productions. The 800-capacity amphitheatre has accommodated 350,000 since 2003, revitalising a centuries-old tradition and knocking down barriers to the stage. There's no need to book, just arrive early for a spot. With street food from the likes of KERB nearby, a Thames-side view of London's architecture, and Potters Fields Park feet away – Scoop is a rarity to be enjoyed.
City Hall, The Queen's Walk, SE1 2AA;
freeopenairtheatre.org

Brixton

Brixton might seem to be at the centre of what's new today, but it has been around since medieval times. More recently, the neighbourhood has been largely shaped by Victorian architecture that came with the extension of the London Underground and the arrival of the West Indian community in the post-war period. The influence is everywhere to see – a mix of grand architecture and a vibrant street culture with Brixton Market at its heart. The market is the place to experience Brixton's food and shopping at it's best, but if you want to find out more about the area's history the Black Cultural Archive is well worth a visit and hosts regular exhibitions by local artists. David Bowie remains Brixton's most famous musical son, and a mural of him just opposite the station attracts his most fervent fans. There's no shortage of places to eat and shop on the main streets, but you can also head south to Herne Hill, where bucolic bookshops and cafés line the road leading to Brockwell Park. The jewel in Brixton's crown, the park offers one of the best vistas of the city and an Art Deco lido for an unmissable day out.

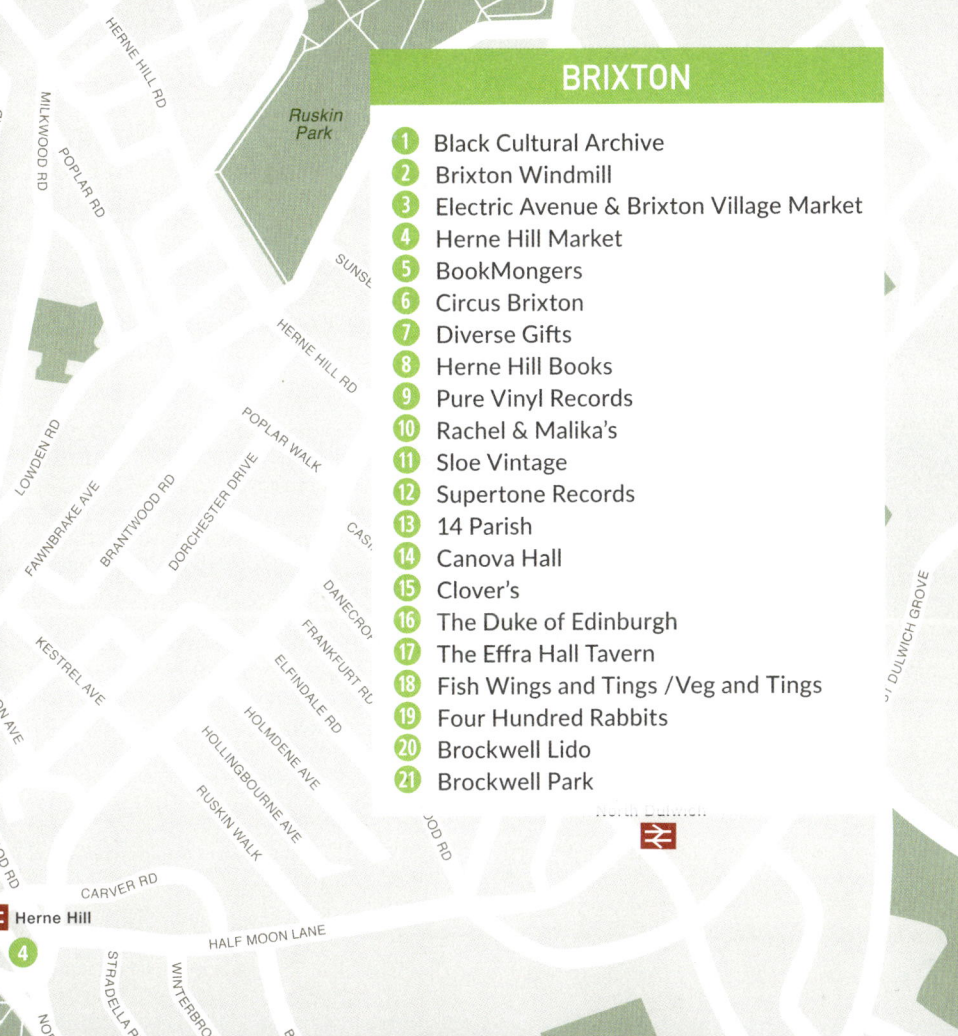

BRIXTON

1. Black Cultural Archive
2. Brixton Windmill
3. Electric Avenue & Brixton Village Market
4. Herne Hill Market
5. BookMongers
6. Circus Brixton
7. Diverse Gifts
8. Herne Hill Books
9. Pure Vinyl Records
10. Rachel & Malika's
11. Sloe Vintage
12. Supertone Records
13. 14 Parish
14. Canova Hall
15. Clover's
16. The Duke of Edinburgh
17. The Effra Hall Tavern
18. Fish Wings and Tings / Veg and Tings
19. Four Hundred Rabbits
20. Brockwell Lido
21. Brockwell Park

Visit

❶ Black Cultural Archive
The home of Black British art

The Black Cultural Archives is a unique cultural space that is deeply rooted in its surroundings. Situated on Windrush Square, this area welcomed the first post-war West Indian migrants in 1948, making it the heart of London's Afro-Caribbean community. In 1998, the square was renamed to commemorate the 50th anniversary of the HMT Empire Windrush's arrival in the UK. Knowing its history makes entering the BCA a powerful experience. It was established following the 1981 Brixton uprising, which was a response to the tragic New Cross house fire that claimed the lives of 13 young Black people. The resulting protest saw placards bearing the words '13 dead and nothing said'. In the wake of this, educationalist and historian Len Garrison recognized the need for a space to preserve and celebrate the history of people of African descent in Britain, and thus the BCA was born. Since then, the Grade-II listed building has served as a platform for discussion, gathering and showcasing art from the African diaspora. Despite the gentrification of Brixton, the BCA remains committed to preserving Windrush Square's status as a place defined by Black history. In a beautiful moment in 2022, 50 artists gathered in the square to mark the 40th anniversary of the UK Black Arts Movement.

Windrush Square, SW2 1EF;
blackculturalarchives.com

❷ Brixton Windmill
London's last working windmill

Built in 1816 and in service under the same family until 1934, Brixton Windmill is a relic of Lambeth's industrious past. Urbanisation, steam and gas power and mass-produced bread led to the demise of the area's eleven other windmills, but Brixton's escaped this fate by transforming into a public garden in the 1950s. Its current purpose as a museum and education centre came about in 2011. As a former industrial building, there are potential dangers to visiting the site, including steep ladders, low beams and heavy machinery, as well as the lack of space, so visitor numbers are restricted and people under 1.2 metres tall cannot go above the first floor. On open days there are short tours of the building that don't require booking, and longer tours with access to the upper floors, which must be booked in advance. Every Saturday morning at 11.30am (weather permitting) they hold a one-hour drop-in tai chi class in the park (pay by donation). A group of volunteers also meets at 1pm on the first Saturday of every month to tend the garden. Facilities include a children's playground, a stay-and-play facility for preschool children and a ping pong table. The events held here are as diverse as a Beer and Bread Festival in May, spring and autumn bat walks, Art in the Park in August, a Harvest Festival in September and Santa in the Windmill every Christmas.

Windmill Gardens, Blenheim Gardens, SW2 5DA;
brixtonwindmill.org

Shop

❸ Electric Avenue & Brixton Village Market
Go-to destination for global goods

Immortalised in the 1983 hit track by Eddy Grant about the Brixton uprising, this vibrant market street was the first to be lit by electricity and has been in operation since the 1880s. Today, it is one of the best places in London to shop for African, Caribbean, South American and Asian goods, spread out over hundreds of different stalls, shops and restaurants and including fresh produce and clothing. Special mention goes to African Queen Fabrics, Harry Otto & Sons fishmongers, Wing Tai's Chinese supermarket and Brixton Wholefoods. Although the elegant cast-iron Edwardian canopies were destroyed during WWII and removed in the 1980s, the history of the area is still on full show in the Grade-II listed covered arcades of Reliance Arcade, Market Row and Granville Arcade, which make up the newly named Brixton Village. Despite the market facing significant challenges over the years and current significant redevelopment, these streets are still the 'soul of Black Britain' and provide welcome respite on a day out in Brixton.

Electric Avenue, SW9 8JX;
brixtonvillage.com

❹ Herne Hill Market
Quieter market for quality goods

As Brixton has become more bijou in the last few years, Herne Hill Market has bloomed into one of London's best places to buy artisanal goods. Despite being dwarfed by famous markets like Brick Lane and Portobello Road, you can get everything you'll need here, plus some welcome extras. There's food of all kinds, from groceries to ready-to-eat; handmade clothes; house plants; a bike repair stall – nearly all needs are catered for. Taking place every Sunday, and with indie shops, cafés and historic pubs like The Commercial surrounding it, this is one of the best ways to get a feel for the area. Plus, trading days often coincide with live music events that happen here throughout the year.

Railton Road, SE24 0JN; weareccfm.com

❺ BookMongers
Nothing fishy about the fiction here

For the bargain-hunting book lover, there aren't many places better than this second-hand bookshop just minutes away from Brixton station. The stock is extensive, with just about every topic covered and all at reasonable prices. One of the shop's main attractions is the owner Patrick and his plethora of animals. Some are no longer with us and are commemorated in artwork on display. This gem of a bookshop has been trading since 1992, and long may it continue to thrive.

439 Coldharbour Lane, SW9 8LN;
bookmongers.com

❻ Circus Brixton
Homeware in the heart of Brixton Village
This shop in the heart of Brixton Village offers an incredible range of gifts and homewares from their small corner site. From affordable posters to higher-end paintings, they have lots of things to beautify your home. Very much a part of the Brixton Village revival, there are both vintage and contemporary items on offer. Run with care by Tabatha, this is definitely a great place to keep in mind when on a trip to Brixton.

79 Brixton Village, SW9 8PS; circusbrixton.com

❼ Diverse Gifts
Local champion of Black-owned businesses
Many will know this colourful shopfront on Coldharbour Lane, but venture inside and you'll discover the offering is even more diverse than you would imagine. What started life as a silver jewellery stall in the 90s has grown into a shop that is full of lifestyle products that reflect the diasporic community of Brixton, that owner Anita calls home. The store is particularly strong on gifts celebrating the area with lots of Brixton related things from fridge magnets to posters and maps. The team pride themselves on ensuring that at least 50% of their products are supplied by Black-owned businesses. There are books, toys, accessories and foodstuffs available too, so all your gift-giving needs are covered.

390 Coldharbour Lane, SW9 8LF
diversegifts.com

❽ Herne Hill Books
Colourful corner bookstore with first-class customer service
This colourful corner bookshop is the sister store of Clapham Books and has been keeping Herne Hill's locals happy with its eclectic range of titles since 2009. The staff are known for their skill at researching and ordering hard-to-find and imported books. A treasure trove for the would-be gift giver and a paradise for the browser. Visiting is a perfect interlude to a day out at the market here or after a wander around the neighbouring park.

289 Railton Road, SE24 0LY;
claphambooks.com

❾ Pure Vinyl Records
One-woman record shop
Pure Vinyl is the love child of Claudia Wilson, who has serious credentials in Brixton as a specialist purveyor of Soul, RnB, Funk, Jazz, Reggae and more. Having established a reputation in Reliance Arcade, she has now moved to The Department Store (a recently revitalised Edwardian shopping complex). The shop may look a little more up-market, but it still draws in a community of locals that come for the expert curation, and occasional events like open deck sessions. T-shirts, posters and tote bags mean if you haven't made your mind up as to what record to buy, you needn't leave empty handed.

246 Ferndale Rd, London SW9 8FR;
thedepartmentstore.com

Brixton - Shop

Brixton - Shop

⑩ Rachel & Malika's
Alladin's cave for African, Asian and South American craftsmanship

This beautiful boutique in the heart of Brixton is the number one place for sourcing gifts for anyone with a passion for African, Asian or South American craftsmanship. It began life a decade ago by importing traditional instruments, including handmade koras from Mali, and has blossomed into one of the most vibrant shops in town. Owners Malika and Kat source all the artisanal goods on sale ethically, so you can rest assured your money is going toward supporting communities in need. Look out for the turquoise façade with all manner of things hung up outside – it's hard to miss inside Brixton Market!
Unit 34, Granville Arcade, Coldharbour Lane, SW9 8PR; rachelandmalikas.com

⑪ Sloe Vintage
Brixton's best secondhand womenswear

For vintage womenswear, look no further. Sloe Vintage is Brixton's best secondhand clothing shop, with the sort of 'Shabby Chic' fashion available at affordable prices. With both designer and unbranded pieces starting around £30, it's not a bulk-buy affair, but you are likely to leave with at least one item for yourself or the young woman in your life, as their selection is expertly curated. In the heart of the market, Sloe Vintage is a worthwhile visit on a day's shopping in Brixton.
38 Brixton Village, SW9 8PR; sloevintage.com

⑫ Supertone Records
Brixton's oldest and best record shop

Supertone Records is one of the last old school vinyl shops in Brixton. It's survival is testament to the owner Wally B, who's been in business since 1984 and survived the digital transition through his friendliness and unrivalled passion for the oldest and best Reggae, Ska and Dub records. Much of his stock are originals that date back to the '60's and as a result are almost impossible to find elsewhere. What's more, the store is just an incredible sight to behold – a true treasure trove of colourful sleeves, that feels like a slice of London from another era.
110 Acre Lane, SW2 5RA; supertonerecords.com

Eat & Drink

⑬ 14 Parish
Inexpensive Caribbean cuisine
A mere £2.50 for a freshly made patty is by far the most economical eat you'll find in Brixton these days. Thankfully, the takeaway-only, 14 Parish have you covered on that front. You'll find a steady stream of customers from the local community coming here each day for these best-in-class baked goods, as well as goat curry, saltfish & ackee, rice & peas, and other Caribbean culinary classics.
424 Coldharbour Lane, SW9 8LF; 14parish.co.uk

⑭ Canova Hall
Dinning hall in a former department store
Although part of a chain, Canova Hall is a good spot for freelancers or work-from-homers to get out of the house for a productive day's work. You can buy a 'Hotdesk Pass' via their app, which gets you bottomless coffee (with no restrictions – cappuccino to espresso, regular or plant-based milk) or other hot drinks to enjoy in their comfortable space, as well as fast WiFi and plentiful sockets. The pass is valid for takeaway drinks too, so it can be a cost-effective alternative to your regular coffee run. They serve Neapolitan-style pizza and pasta, and a bottomless brunch on weekends. Found inside a renovated Edwardian department store, Canova Hall is a vast and impressive eatery with outside seating on fine days.
250 Ferndale Road, SW9 8BQ; canovahall.com

⑮ Clover's
Brixton's neighbourhood café since 1999
Only a stone's throw from Brixton's main drag, Clover's is a neighbourhood bar and restaurant that serves great coffee, comfort food and cocktails. Formerly Lounge – a long-standing Brixton institution – this spot has the same ownership and community feel, and offers something for everyone. The menu includes favourites like fritters, jerk chicken and plantain, Halloumi and falafel wraps and great cooked breakfasts. It's just as good for grabbing a drink and watching the world go by from the large windows within its simple Danish-style interior.
58 Atlantic Road, SW9 8PY

Brixton - Eat & Drink

⓰ The Duke of Edinburgh
A big pub with an even bigger beer garden

This Grade-II listed pub is another local favourite, not least for the fact it has South London's largest beer garden, in which you can get great BBQ food and enjoy the sun. If the weather doesn't allow this, then the pool table and live sports coverage inside are two other attractions that keep a loyal crowd of customers coming every night of the week, guaranteeing good vibes for any would-be visitors. The Duke is a youthful place, so not necessarily where to go if with kids or for a quiet pint, but dogs are encouraged and it's far friendlier and more authentic than most of the other pubs in the area.

204 Ferndale Rd, SW9 8AG;
dukeofedinburghpub.com

⓱ The Effra Hall Tavern
A noisy but great neighbourhood pub

Effra Hall is everything you'd want from a neighbourhood pub. It's an impressive historic building, with a ghost sign to prove it, but more than that it's popular with locals. A lot of this has to do with the live music they play four nights a week, ranging from ska to jazz and always boisterous, as well as the Caribbean food they serve alongside it. The inside features a horseshoe bar and framed cigarette cards on the walls, as well as screens for watching sports. Bear in mind that their no kids, no canines policy means the Effra Hall is strictly for grown-up fun.

38A Kellett Road, SW2 1EB

⓲ Fish Wings & Tings / Veg & Tings
Brixton's Caribbean culinary king

The colourful shop fronts of these two neighbouring restaurants are the first things you see as you enter Granville Arcade. Brian Danclair has been serving up Caribbean classics like oxtail, jerk chicken and curry mutton here for over a decade. Now, he also runs a vegetarian establishment, serving up dishes like Doubles – a Trinidadian street food dish of flatbread with curried chickpeas – and Ital stew, packed with veggies, rice and beans. Indoor and outdoor seating means you can opt for what suits depending on the weather and if you are after a sit-down dinner, rest assured the rum punch flows as freely as the food.

Brixton Village, 3 Granville Arcade, Coldharbour Lane, SW9 8PR; fishwingsandtings.co.uk

⓳ Four Hundred Rabbits
Food at the lido is a local favourite

Adjacent to the Grade-II listed lido is one of Brixton's most enjoyable eateries – a café that is every bit as Art Deco as its surroundings, and now hosts a successful pizzeria. Sourdough bases and wood fired ovens ensure it feels like a treat after bracing the cold of the pool outside. There are plenty of veggie, vegan and GF options, plus a hearty brunch and gelato should you fancy something sweet. Indoor and outdoor seating mean you can dine whatever the weather.

The Lido Café, Dulwich Road, SE24 0PA; 400rabbits.co.uk

Outdoors

⓴ Brockwell Lido
Art Deco masterpiece
This much-loved landmark has been at the heart of the local community since 1937, when it replaced the natural bathing ponds in the park. Although it fell into disuse for a few years, two former council employees saved it, and with the help of some crowdfunding it's been going strong since, being given Grade-II listed status in 2003. Once you visit, it's easy to see why. The Moderne-style building is a lesson in symmetry that exudes a luxurious egalitarianism characteristic of the utopian ideals of the time. Meanwhile, the 50m outdoor pool is always teeming with activity, especially so during the summer months, when the Lido becomes one of the most popular sights for South Londoners looking to cool off from or soak up the sun. With recently installed gym equipment plus an extensive programme of group exercise classes on offer, there's not much more you could ask for from a leisure centre. Really, what makes the Lido special are the dedicated swimmers that attend. Their enthusiastic campaigning has secured it is open all year round for the 'Icicles' who brave the (unheated) winter months here, as well as those who enjoy the newly installed poolside sauna, water polo and café facilities.
Brockwell Park, Dulwich Road, SE24 0PA;
brockwelllido.com

㉑ Brockwell Park
Brixton's best and biggest park
Brockwell Park has been providing panoramic views to the public since 1892, although undoubtedly the vista today is a more dramatic one, since London's skyline has erupted in the last few decades. It's big enough to feel alone in, except in summer when sunbathers seek out its exposed slopes, or else during the Lambeth Country Show and fireworks displays here, in July and November respectively. Recent restoration has attracted occasional outdoor theatre performances, as well as an improved children's playground, community greenhouses that host workshops especially suited to families, and a serene walled rose garden perfect for contemplation. For those looking to be more active, tennis courts, a football pitch, a bowling green and a basketball court are all popular options, but none more so than the adjacent Art Deco lido. At the top of the hill, you'll find what was Brockwell Hall, and now hosts the park's café. There are 125 acres to explore, all of which are designated as a Site of Importance for Nature Conservation. It's little wonder over 4 million visitors come here each year to escape the grind of the Big Smoke – it's the perfect focal point for a day out in Brixton.
Brockwell Park, SE24 0NG;
friendsofbrockwellpark.org

Greenwich

Greenwich is a UNESCO World Heritage Site with a history dating back to the Tudor kings and queens who favoured the then-rural area for their pleasure palaces, around what is now Greenwich Park. But more than any monarch, it was Christopher Wren who left the most visibly enduring legacy. The architect's fingerprint is recognisable in the Old Royal Naval College and Royal Observatory, two destinations you must visit. Along with seeing two of the most beautiful and historically fascinating buildings in the country, from the Observatory you can enjoy one of London's best views. You're spoilt for choice with beauty and history, as many other museums and manors surround the park. If you've had your sightseeing fix, the nearby market is a great place for contemporary crafts, gifts and street food from around the world. If you still want to fill up on history, head to Goddard's for a plate of pie, mash and maybe eels; a 19th century classic of English cuisine. To get the full maritime experience, you can arrive or depart on a Thames Clipper boat. They're not quite the Cutty Sark, but are a surprisingly cheap and convenient way of visiting this unique neighbourhood.

GREENWICH

1. Cutty Sark
2. The Fan Museum
3. National Maritime Museum
4. Old Royal Naval College and The Painted Hall
5. Queen's House
6. Ranger's House
7. Royal Observatory Greenwich & Peter Harrison Planetarium
8. Casbah Records
9. Greenwich Market
10. The Junk Shop
11. Royal Hill
12. Goddards at Greenwich
13. Greenwich Market Food Hall
14. Heap's Gourmet Sausages
15. Naked Coffee
16. Pavilion Café
17. The Prince of Greenwich
18. Trafalgar Tavern
19. Greenwich Park

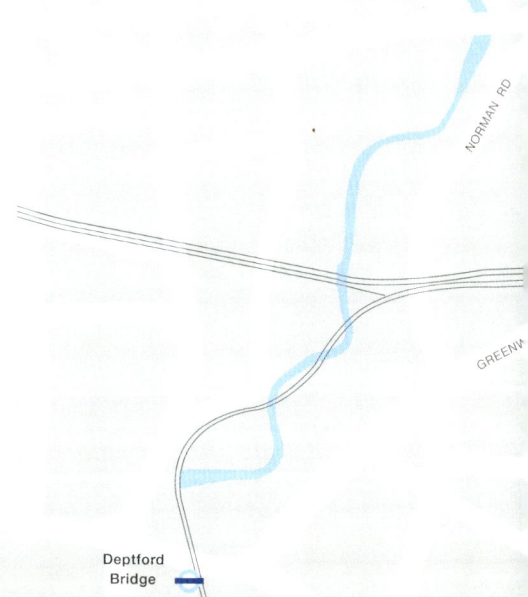

Visit

❶ Cutty Sark
Britain's only original 19th-century clipper ship

Launched in 1869, the *Cutty Sark* is the last surviving tea clipper. This record-breaking merchant vessel sailed over a million nautical miles during her seafaring days before settling in Greenwich in the 1950s. £50 million saved her from a fire in 2007, so you can now walk beneath her sleek copper-clad hull through a glass-covered dry dock. Deep in the hold, where 10,000 tea chests would have once been stowed, displays tell the history of the tea trade. On the upper deck, you can admire the gleaming brassware, pristine winding gears and neatly coiled ropes that were essential to the running of the ship. At one end of the Dry Berth, you'll find the world's largest collection of ship figureheads. This colourful but eerie display dates mainly from the 19th century and includes historic figures such as Florence Nightingale, Gladstone and Disraeli, all of whom are overseen by Nannie, the formidable witch that served as *Cutty Sark's* figurehead.

King William Walk, SE10 9HT;
rmg.co.uk

❷ The Fan Museum
The history of fans

Inside two Georgian houses, this dainty museum oozes gentility. The permanent display explores the history of fan-making and includes a rare 17th-century example depicting a royal birthday party at the court of King Louis XIV. The fans are crafted from unlikely materials, from tortoiseshell, ivory and mother of pearl to Welsh slate. Recent high-profile acquisitions include a fan leaf painted by Gauguin and one by Sickert featuring a music hall scene. Regularly changing exhibitions upstairs showcase fans from the museum's 4000-strong collection, highlighting particular themes. Previous shows have covered the Belle Epoque, advertising fans and Chinese exports. In 2023 the museum curated a royal exhibition to coincide with the coronation. They also run fan-making workshops and can produce fans to order for special occasions. Meanwhile, the museum shop includes fanfare like specially commissioned jewellery, greeting cards, toiletries, tea cosies, specialist publications and of course a variety of fans.

12 Crooms Hill, SE10 8ER;
thefanmuseum.org.uk

❸ National Maritime Museum
The world's largest maritime museum

The largest maritime museum in the world explores 500 years of salt-encrusted British history, from the swashbuckling of Walter Raleigh to the work of Sir Richard Attenborough and the British Antarctic Survey. First opened to the public in 1937, you enter via the Sammy Ofer Wing, past Yinka Shonibare's landmark sculpture *Nelson's Ship in a Bottle*. The first Voyagers gallery showcases 200 relics of our relationship with the sea, from sailors' love tokens to remains of the Titanic. Family activities include map-making, while the art curious can see the largest collection of William Hodges paintings in the world – the artist who assisted Captain Cook's voyage. Further on, there are some remarkable artefacts in the collection, such as the uniform worn by Nelson at Trafalgar, Ernest Shackleton's equipment from his treacherous Arctic exploration and paraphernalia of the Merchant Navy, especially from World War I. If all this hasn't left you seasick, the museum café is on deck to provide refreshments.
Romney Road, SE10 9NF;
rmg.co.uk

❹ Old Royal Naval College & The Painted Hall
Most celebrated building in Britain

The centrepiece of the Maritime Greenwich World Heritage Site, this Grade I listed Christopher Wren masterpiece is in UNESCO's words the 'finest and most dramatically sited architectural and landscape ensemble in the British Isles'. Originally constructed as the Royal Hospital for Seamen at Greenwich between 1696 and 1712, the site was later known as Greenwich Hospital. It closed as a hospital in 1869 and then functioned as the Royal Naval College from 1873 until 1998. It sits atop the site of Greenwich Palace: the birthplace of Henry VIII, Mary I and Elizabeth I and before then a significant royal pleasure palace. Since 2002, the entire College has been open to the public daily, everything free of charge except for The Painted Hall which is ticketed and is certainly the pièce de résistance for visitors. Painted between 1707 and 1726 by Sir James Thornhill, it is London's answer to the Michaelangelo fresco in Rome's Sistine Chapel. 40,000 square feet of Baroque walls and ceilings are covered in striking images of kings, queens and mythological creatures. Originally intended as an eating space for the Greenwich Pensioners who lived at the Royal Hospital, it has in the last decade undergone significant conservation work to ensure it remains a public attraction for years to come.
Old Royal Naval College, SE10 9NN;
ornc.org

❺ The Queen's House
England's first classical building
Designed by the pioneering Inigo Jones for James I's wife Anne of Denmark, this royal residence holds the double distinction of being the first Classical building in England and the first to have a cantilevered staircase. Completed in 1638, Anne sadly never got to see the finished building, dying of tuberculosis in 1619. The King and Queen's Presence Chambers are studded with paintings of the building's historic residents. Many works by masters like Reynolds, Hogarth and Turner are in the gallery and the painted ceiling *An Allegory of Peace and the Arts* by Orazio and Artemisia Gentileschis rivals the neighbouring painted hall. A must-visit enclave of hidden British masterworks.
Romney Road, SE10 9NF; rmg.co.uk

❻ Ranger's House – Wernher Collection
A Randlord's regal personal collection
This Georgian villa and former royal residence is an opulent assembly of objets d'art amassed by Sir Julius Wernher in the 19th and early 20th centuries. He made his fortune in the South African gold and diamond industries. The displays cover 12 rooms and include bronze statuary, medieval ivories, Old Masters, Renaissance jewellery, Sèvres porcelain and majolica ceramics. It's a remarkable collection including works by Hoppner, Romney and Reynolds. Tucked away at the top of Greenwich Park, it's easily missed but well worth seeking out.
Chesterfield Walk, SE10 8QX;
english-heritage.org.uk

❼ Royal Observatory Greenwich & Peter Harrison Planetarium
Museum at the centre of time and space

Straddling the Meridian line at 0 degrees longitude and home of Greenwich Mean Time, the Royal Observatory can call itself the centre of time and space. Visitors play with this by taking photographs with one foot on either side of the line. Other highlights of the observatory include the Camera Obscura, which projects a revolving panorama of Greenwich; Flamsteed House, containing the spartan apartments of the Astronomers Royal; and the Octagon Room, a rare Christopher Wren designed domestic interior. The display of instruments for measuring time and space includes the timepiece that solved the navigators' problem of assessing longitude, John Harrison's H4 chronometer – the most important timekeeper ever made. Visitors can step inside the dome of the Great Equatorial Telescope (completed in 1893 and one of the largest of its kind in the world) and at 1pm look out for the dropping Time Ball, which enabled ships on the Thames to set their chronometers. The Planetarium has a free exhibition exploring Mars, with displays of early drawings and photographs taken by contemporary rovers. If the red planet whets your appetite, the Planetarium's ticketed shows follow the birth and life of a star and offer guidance from a real astronomer on what to see in the sky that night.

Blackheath Avenue, SE10 8XJ;
rmg.co.uk

Shop

❽ Casbah Records
Established Greenwich vinyl store

The instantly recognisable yellow sign with its psychedelic font is one of the most recognisable shop fronts on Creek Road. It's also stocked full of exotic treasures just waiting to be discovered. The owners, the Davis brothers, started out on Greenwich Market in the 1980s, with the current shop having been in operation since 2009. 40 years in the trade means they've got unparalleled expertise on how to source and sell a massive stock of records from all genres. Alongside wax, they've got books, DVDs, tapes, comics (both new and old), as well as their own t-shirts, totes and badges. On Record Store Day in late April each year, they open especially at midnight for queuers to get their hands on limited-edition vinyl – someone once snagged themselves a first pressing of Led Zeppelin's first album with turquoise lettering for £1,500 here.

320-322 Creek Road, SE10 9SW;
casbahrecords.co.uk

❾ Greenwich Market
London market in a World Heritage Site

Between 10am and 5.30pm daily, one of London's oldest markets carries on as it has since it acquired a royal charter in 1700, although the fruit and veg has been replaced by arts, crafts, collectables and food. Set in the World Heritage Site of Maritime Greenwich, other additions to the original courtyard of cobbled stones and paving include a glass roof and a modern food court. This latter feature has become increasingly significant in recent years as street food has come to dominate around a quarter of the market's overall trade, especially around College Approach. The weekend is still mostly a mix of craft goods, whilst Thursdays and Fridays see more vintage items on offer. If you've exhausted the second-hand options in the market, then shops surrounding the courtyard like Joli Vintage Living and Music & Video Exchange offer a comparable treasure trove to explore.

Greenwich Church Street, SE10 9HZ;
greenwichmarket.london

Greenwich - Shop

🔟 The Junk Shop
One person's trash is another's treasure
This antique shop is as close to Dr Who's Tardis as can be – larger on the inside than the outside. Established in 1954, it's a stalwart of antiques in Greenwich, and has survived when so many similar businesses have disappeared. The basement is separated into 14 distinct units, which are rented to artists and traders. A shop that takes the adage 'One person's trash is another's treasure' quite literally, they stock items obtained from house clearances, including rusty fireplaces, Edwardian children's beds, and other curiosities. The assortment of goods is vast, ranging from porcelain dogs and vintage radios to croquet sets and a captain's uniform. If all this shopping makes you thirsty, Naked Coffee have a hatch at the front of the shop that should hit the spot (see p.242).

9 Greenwich South Street, SE10 8NW;
junkshopandspreadeagleantiques.co.uk

🔼 Royal Hill
Residential road turned shopping street
Just around the corner from Greenwich rail station on the walk towards Maritime Greenwich, you'll find a street full of Georgian houses and the impossible-to-miss Art Deco town hall with its clock tower. Along the road are several noteworthy independent businesses that fulfil most shopping needs. Ellis and Jones supply the fish; The Cheeseboard has all the dairy; Drings is a top traditional butcher; and The Creaky Shed is the only local greengrocer left in Greenwich. Further along, there are pubs and cafés, but a few will be amused by Maritime Books – London's only specialist naval and maritime bookshop, which boasts 12,000-15,000 titles including second-hand and antiquarian copies.

Royal Hill, SE10 8RT

Greenwich - Eat & Drink

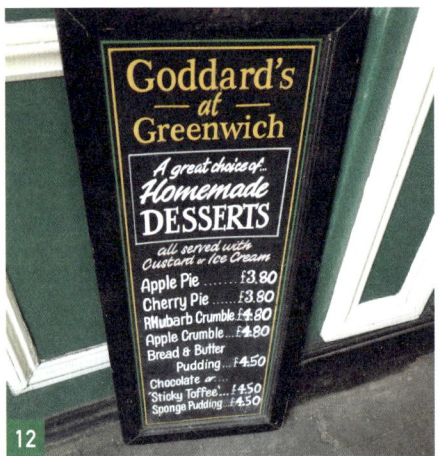

Eat & Drink

⓬ Goddards at Greenwich
19th century pie & mash shop

Few family-run businesses can claim to have been going since 1890, although those that do will invariably be pie and mash shops. This Cockney classic is fast becoming extinct in the East End thanks to gentrification and development, but vestiges of it remain in south London. Adapting to the times, you can find new filling choices like chicken & ham or cheese & onion, but what you really come for is the minced beef with mash and parsley liquor, as well as some steamed or jellied eels. This historic cuisine has kept Londoners well-fed for centuries, as have hearty puddings like bread & butter or sticky toffee with custard. It's a cosy place to eat with traditional wooden booths where locals now vie for space with tourists, looking to experience authentic English food while exploring Greenwich.

22 King William Walk, SE10 9HU;
goddardsatgreenwich.co.uk

⓭ Greenwich Market Food Hall
Greenwich's global gourmet offering

Greenwich Market is well-known for its varied arts and crafts, but has recently developed a street food scene too. The stalls are divided into two parts, with most in the main body of the market at the College Approach entrance, and a food court at the Greenwich Church Street entrance. If shopping gives you an appetite then you'll be spoilt for choice between cuisines from all over the world. There's everything here from Argentinian empanadas to Ethiopian injera, so you can satisfy just about any craving. The food court has seating, so you can take a pew to enjoy your food in comfort.

Greenwich Church Street, SE10 9HZ;
greenwichmarket.london

⓮ Heap's Gourmet Sausages & Farm Shop
The supreme sausage sandwich

The brainchild of gourmet sausage master Martin Heap and his business partner Vincenzo Carbonara, this farm shop offers a huge range of sausages and other meat products to buy or have served in a bap to enjoy on the go. It's mostly a takeaway service, but there is outdoor seating and the shop is right by one of the entrances to Greenwich Park, so you can easily find a patch of grass and enjoy your food while it's still hot. Of course, you can get a cuppa to go with your sarnie, and even a scoop of Hackney gelato for those with a sweet tooth.

8 Nevada Street, SE10 9JL;
heapssausages.com

⑮ Naked Coffee
High-quality coffee and cake from a hatch
A glass hatch at the front entrance of a junk shop might not sound like the standard place for getting your caffeine fix, but Naked Coffee defies expectations with their selection of drinks and cakes. The friendly staff and location away from the high street give a lovely neighbourhood feel to the place. Any visit here would be incomplete without at least a quick peruse of the adjoining Junk Shop (see p.239).

9 Greenwich South Street, SE10 8NW;
nakedmade.co.uk

⑯ The Pavilion Café
The perfect park café
If you've walked up the steep incline of Greenwich Park to pay your respects to General Wolfe or visit the Observatory, you will likely be in need of some refreshment. The Pavilion Café is perfectly placed, just behind both attractions in its own grounds with lots of outdoor seating. The bright-white, hexagonal building was first opened in 1906. Inside, it is modern and light following a major refurb in 2024. The café is part of the Benugo group, and offers freshly made dishes and coffee. It's a great place to relax before continuing your exploration of the park.

Charlton Way, SE10 8QY;
benugo.com

⑰ The Prince of Greenwich
Local's pub where everyone's welcome
This old Victorian pub used to be called The Albert, but was revamped and reopened as The Prince of Greenwich in 2015. The owner, Pietro La Rosa, runs the place with ebullient charm, creating what he calls a 'museum pub', with lots of cosy sofas and art that add to the atmosphere. Pietro doubles as the chef, and the pub has acquired a reputation for its excellent Italian food. Sundays are best for enjoying live music, but any day will give you a flavour of the real Greenwich.

72 Royal Hill, SE10 8RT;
theprinceofgreenwichpub.com

⑱ Trafalgar Tavern
Victorian pub with a nautical theme
This vast riverside pub was built in 1837 – the same year Victoria ascended the throne. Mentioned in *Our Mutual Friend*, this was a favourite haunt of Dickens, who like Wilkie Collins, Macaulay and Thackeray came here for the famous whitebait dinners (which you can still enjoy). Maritime scenes and portraits of the likes of admirals Nelson, Hardy and Howe adorn the walls. The place has a traditional feel and the nautical theme is helped by the Thames lapping against the walls. The place is huge with a terrace guarded by a statue of Horatio, so you needn't worry about finding somewhere to sit. A picture-perfect place for a pint after perusing the royal park.

Park Row, SE10 9NW;
trafalgartavern.co.uk

Outdoors

🔟 Greenwich Park
The oldest enclosed Royal Park

Dating to 1427, the oldest enclosed Royal Park really came to life during the youth of Henry VIII, who enjoyed hunting here and introduced deer whose descendants still roam the 183-acre grounds today. James I later enclosed the park; formal gardens followed in the 1660s, and public access was finally allowed in the 18th century. Since then, early Stone Age tools have been discovered, as has evidence of Roman and Viking settlements. Asides from the surrounding architecture of Maritime Greenwich, this is also the starting point of the London Marathon. Would-be explorers should make a beeline for the observatory, which offers a vista atop the hill that is almost unparalleled in its vantage of inner London's skyline: Canary Wharf, the Millennium Dome and St Paul's Cathedral provide a backdrop to the Old Royal Naval College. History buffs should also locate Queen Elizabeth's Oak – a now-dead tree that dates from the 12th century, which Henry VIII danced around with Anne Boleyn and under which Elizabeth I rested.

Greenwich Park, SE10 8QY;
royalparks.co.uk

West

Notting Hill
Richmond
Hammersmith & Chiswick

Notting Hill

Notting Hill was an impoverished neighbourhood for much of its history, especially during the postwar period when slum landlords and Teddy Boys preyed upon recent arrivals from the West Indies. Though tragic, this catalysed slum clearances, the construction of Brutalist icons like the Westway and Trellick Tower, and the birth of Notting Hill Carnival, now one of the capital's most famous annual events. Portobello Road and its world famous market is at the heart of any visit to Notting Hill, at its busiest on Saturdays. Meanwhile, the vintage clothing market under the Westway is just as good on Fridays, with a more relaxed atmosphere. At the north end of the market is Golborne Road, where antique shops and junk stalls join popular places to eat like Lisboa Patisserie – a landmark Portuguese café that serves the best pastel de nata in London. It's a reminder that this part of town is not only home to a sizable West Indian community but also an established Portuguese and Spanish contingent, that combine to create a uniquely diverse neighbourhood. This diversity is well represented in the local businesses, such as the renowned Garcia's deli, open since 1957. A day out in Notting Hill is best when it spills over the borders into the surrounds of Kensington. Here you'll find unmissable museums and green spaces, from the Japanese garden in Holland Park to the Moorish fantasia of Leighton House, as well as much-loved pubs like The Cow on Westbourne Park Road. For beautiful architecture, unique shops and exceptional eateries, Notting Hill is undeniably one of London's best neighbourhoods.

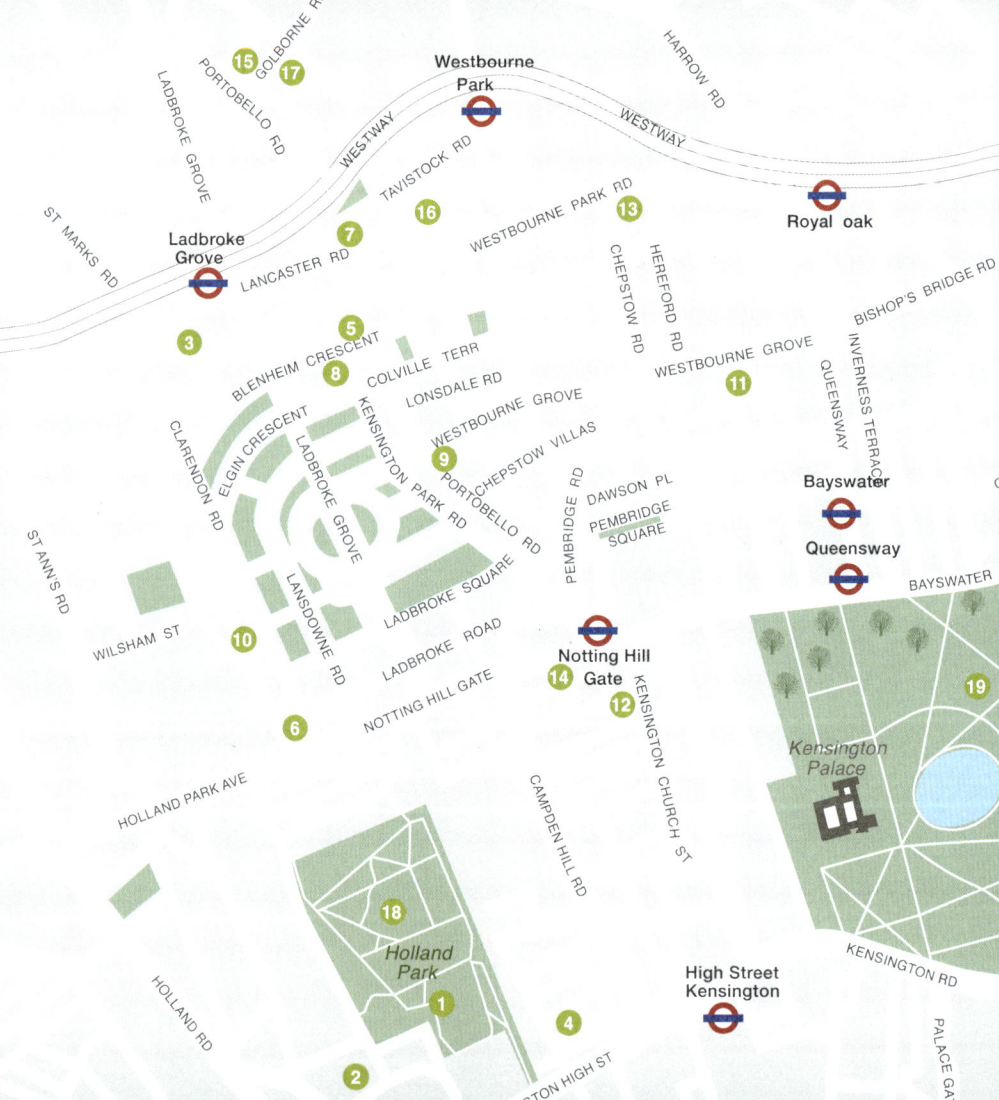

NOTTING HILL

1. Design Museum
2. Leighton House
3. Museum of Brands
4. Sambourne House
5. Books for Cooks
6. Daunt Books
7. Garcia's Food & Wine of Spain
8. L & R Bookshop (Daunt Books)
9. Portobello Road Market
10. Portland Road
11. Al Waha
12. The Churchill Arms
13. The Cow
14. Da Maria
15. Golborne Bistro
16. Jay Dees Catering
17. Lisboa Patisserie
18. Holland Park
19. Kensington Gardens

Visit

❶ Design Museum
A shrine to design
A shrine to contemporary design and architecture, the Design Museum is, with its swooping paraboloid roof, a west London landmark. Since first opening in Shad Thames in 1989 it has championed the role of good design and showcased the work of designers such as Charles and Ray Eames, Zaha Hadid and Sir Paul Smith. The museum's features iconic designs ranging from an AK-47 to Lady Gaga's bin-bag dress. In 2016, it relocated to the beautifully renovated former Commonwealth institute, designed by architect John Pawson. The new home is a masterpiece of concrete, wood, and steel, allowing the museum to expand its reach. Notable exhibitions include the 2019 retrospective of Stanley Kubrick's life and work. The permanent exhibition narrates the story of influential designs from the Industrial Revolution to the present. It highlights designers who have shaped London's aesthetic and practical landscape, such as David Mellor's traffic light and the British road signage system by Kinneir and Calvert. It also showcases the evolution of industrialisation and manufacturing, featuring exhibits like the Model T Ford, robotic arms, and 3D printers. The final section evokes nostalgia, presenting beloved items like the first iMac bubble computer, Sony Walkman, Olivetti Valentine typewriter, and a Dieter Rams record player.
Kensington High Street, W8 6NQ;
designmuseum.org

❷ Leighton House
Victorian house with Islamic interiors
Fresh from an £8 million refurbishment, this evocative haute-bohemian pad was once home to Frederic, Lord Leighton, the great classical painter of the Victorian age. Hung with paintings by the man himself and his Pre-Raphaelite pals Millais and Burne-Jones, and with ceramics by William de Morgan, the house was designed as a palace devoted to art, and its opulent interiors are spellbinding. Leighton's vast studio dominates the upper floor with its high ceiling and large north-facing windows that flood the space with natural light. The domed Arab Hall is the centrepiece of the house: a Moorish fantasia complete with gilt mosaic frieze, antique Iznik tiles, lattice-work Mashrabiya windows and a fountain. A hugely successful artist in his day, Leighton entertained the great and good of the Victorian art world in his flamboyant home but it is instructive to compare the splendour of the public rooms with the austere simplicity of Leighton's sparsely furnished bedroom. Don't forget to visit the new café that looks over the gorgeous gardens.
12 Holland Park Road, W14 8LZ;
rbkc.gov.uk/museums

❸ Museum of Brands
Museum dedicated to the art of consumerism

This delightfully eccentric museum is the brainchild of Robert Opie and pays affectionate homage to 20th century consumerism or, as the Wombles would have it, the 'everyday things that folks leave behind'. Robert Opie's started at the age of 16 with a Munchies' wrapper and since then his collection has grown to comprise thousands of items, including toys, packaging, and advertising artwork. The permanent collection is laid out as a timeline that snakes its way from the 1890s to the present day and provokes delighted cries of recognition as visitors re-encounter the toys, sweets and games of their childhood.

Nostalgia aside, the collection deftly shows how consumerism reflects society, unerringly charting trends like our national obsession with crisps, ready meals and washing whiter than white. Commercial artwork is a particular strength of the collection and the flowing Art Nouveau lines of an Edwardian biscuit tin, or the striking Art Deco cover of a 1920s Radio Times show how the art movements of the day affected the look of ephemeral everyday items. The displays of vintage fashions have been expanded and reflect Opie's view of clothing as the ultimate human packaging. The shop stocks an appealing range of nostalgic products and the tearoom has a garden, with lush plants and outdoor seating.

111-117 Lancaster Road, W11 1QT;
museumofbrands.com

❹ Sambourne House
The place behind Punch

Remarkably preserved and complete with its original interior decoration and contents, Sambourne House is one of London's best-kept secrets. From 1875, this time capsule of a terraced house was the home of Punch illustrator and cartoonist Edward Linley Sambourne and his family. Originally decorated by him in keeping with fashionable aesthetic principles, the interiors evolved into wonderfully eclectic artistic statements within the confines of a then-typical middle-class home. The house is jam-packed with pictures, ornaments and knick-knacks. Each room tells a story, from the elegant drawing room to the charming bedrooms, and you can easily imagine the lives of the Victorian family who once lived here. But the true highlight is the cartoonist Edward Linley's studio, which has been restored to its former glory and offers a fascinating insight into his creative process through the intricate sketches and drawings on display. The guided tour of the house is led by their knowledgeable and enthusiastic staff, providing a wealth of information about the house's history and its former residents.

18 Stafford Terrace, W8 7BH;
rbkc.gov.uk/museums

Shop

❺ Books for Cooks
London's only Cookbook shop

Opened in 1983, this shop is possibly the most famous cookery bookshop in the world. It has more than eight thousand titles (including rare and out-of-print volumes) and is a place of pilgrimage for foodies from across the globe. The shop sells books on all aspects of food, from specialist professional manuals to family cookbooks. There is a delightful café at the back, where a rota of chefs prepare cookbook recipes. A remarkable bookshop and one all London foodies should visit. Opposite, you'll find the Notting Hill Bookshop (at 13 Blenheim Crescent), that was a location in the film *Notting Hill*.

4 Blenheim Crescent, W11 1NN;
booksforcooks.com

❻ Daunt Books
Elegant branch of this London Chain

Anyone in London will be familiar with Daunt Books with branches all over the city. The Holland Park branch is a particularly large and well stocked store with an elegant Georgian shop front that always encourages passers by to drop in for a browse. They offer a good selection of the current bestsellers and talked about books and can order more obscure titles for next day delivery. A definite must visit for book worms visiting the area.

112-114 Holland Park Avenue, W11 4UA;
dauntbooks.co.uk

7 Garcia's Food & Wine of Spain
A Mecca for Iberian food

On the corner of Tavistock Road close to the Westway, Garcia's Spanish deli is easily missed on a busy market day when the stalls obscure its impressive frontage. But the shop is a must visit for anyone who likes Spanish food. The fragrance of the shop is an experience in itself. You're guaranteed to find the best Spanish cured meats, specialty rice, fresh pastries and wine, as well as expert help and friendly service. It's a welcome reminder that this part of town also has a large Spanish population that keeps this independent shop busy as the source for all the best produce from their homeland.

248-250 Portobello Road, W11 1LL;
rgarciaandsons.com

8 L & R Bookshop (Daunt Books)
Unique independent bookshop

Founded by the literary agents Sarah Lutyens and Felicity Rubinstein, this store is a love affair to book shopping from an industry insider's perspective, so alongside a great stock of fiction and non-fiction titles, you can enjoy sitting down in comfortable furniture and enjoy a browse. Best of all is their 'A Year in Books' subscription service, where you're sent a beautifully wrapped book each month. The store is now part of the Daunt Books group, but has kept the feel of an independent.

21 Kensington Park Road, W11 2EU;
dauntbooks.co.uk

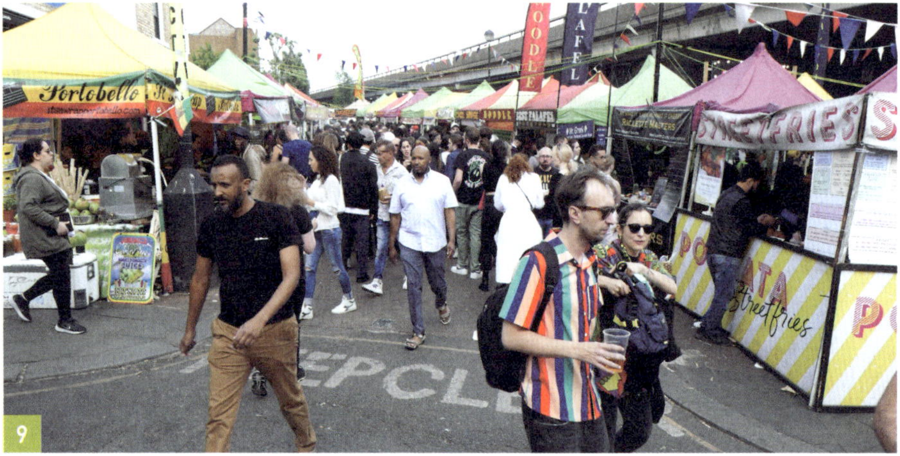
9
Portobello
STREETFRIES
POTATA
Streetfries

9

ALICE'S
THE BEST VALUE IN THE BRITISH ISLES
THE AERONAUTS
PORTOBELLO ROAD W.11
ADMIRALS TAVERN
ROYAL YACHTSMEN
9

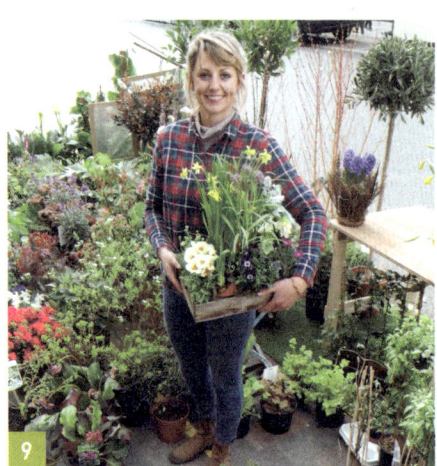

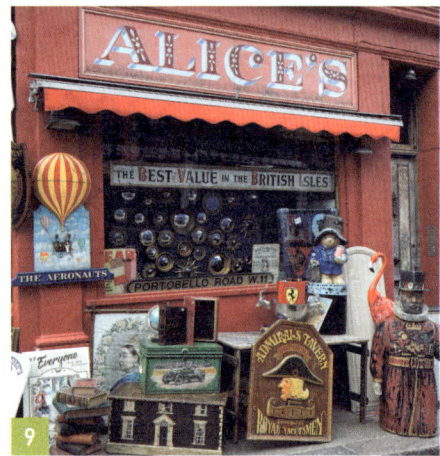

Notting Hill - Shop

⑨ Portobello Road Market
West London's most famous market

Portobello Road is one of London's most famous streets – and is featured in films like *Notting Hill* and *Paddington*, in books like Martin Amis's *London Fields*, and in songs by musicians as varied as Caetano Veloso and Blur. Since the 18th century, it has been a destination by virtue of its many shops, restaurants and of course the Saturday antiques market, which is the largest in London. Hundreds of dealers show up to sell to thousands of tourists, creating a noisy, mile-long procession that snakes beyond the Westway. The southern end has genuine antiques for the affluent crowd, whilst the northern end has vintage clothes to be dug out under the canopy of Portobello Green Market, with plenty of street food and fresh produce in between. The market runs the entire length of Notting Hill and onto Goldborne Road with the soaring Trellick Tower in the distance. A Saturday sojourn down the Portobello is one of London's great experiences. Some shops on or next to Portobello Road you shouldn't miss are Les Couilles du Chien (long-running antique shop); One Of A Kind Fashion Archive (archive of iconic designer pieces); Found and Vision and Rellik (second-hand designer labels); and Garcia's Food and Wine (see p.257).

Portobello Road, W11 1LJ;
portbelloroad.co.uk

⑩ Portland Road
Street full of upmarket speciality shops

Portland Road tells the story of changing London. Built by speculative developers in the 1850s on a strip of land containing the Potteries and Piggeries, one of the most notorious slums in London, it has since become one of the most expensive places to buy a house in London. If you're wandering in the area, it's well worth checking out the pedestrianised part of the street, where a number of upmarket specialty shops have been trading for the last few decades. If in need of fine tableware, Summerill & Bishop is an evangelist for a well-laid table. Meanwhile, The Cross and Myriad are two shops run by female entrepreneurs, that sell high-end fashion and antiques, respectively.

Portland Road, W11 4LQ

Eat & Drink

⓫ Al Waha
An oasis for Lebanese cuisine
It would be remiss not to reflect West London's significant Arab community, but Al Waha makes that easy. Translating to 'oasis', it is the place to go for Lebanese cooking in the capital, with dishes like samakeh harrah – a spicy sea bass speciality – joining more familiar classics like tabbouleh, falafel, mezze and mixed grill. A sit-down affair, you can indulge in a bottle of wine and enjoy the attentive service at this long-standing local institution.
75 Westbourne Grove, W2 4UL

⓬ The Churchill Arms
London's most photogenic boozer
The first thing you notice about this pub is the flowers. Many thousands of them cover every inch of the exterior, making for one of the most remarkable sights in the city. The inside is just as remarkable – jam-packed with memorabilia, from pictures of Churchill and Spitfires to portraits of other world leaders and sporting knick-knacks in between. Just as popular with locals as tourists owing to the lineup of Fuller's beer and Thai curries, it's well worth popping in for a pint after taking a picture.
119 Kensington Church Street, W8 7LN;
churchillarmskensington.co.uk

⓭ The Cow
Bovine goes boho at celebrity-favourite pub
Undoubtedly the coolest pub in West London, The Cow is the creation of Tom Conran (son of Terence) and is a regular haunt for local celebs like Stella McCartney, David Beckham and even Tom Cruise. Why? Well, the cooking is famously good – pints of prawns, crab tagliolini and seafood platters join traditional indulgences like pies, oysters and great Guinness, making for hearty and delicious bar food. But that's the point here – the place is simultaneously bourgeois and unpretentious. Downstairs seating is small tables, stools, a chalkboard menu and no reservations. Upstairs is smarter but just as much fun. The walls are filled with oddities, from vintage beer memorabilia to a large Bosch-like mural populated with regulars, all of which adds to the atmosphere of this proper pub.
89 Westbourne Park Road, W2 5QH;
thecowlondon.com

Notting Hill - Eat & Drink

15

17

17

⑭ Da Maria
Napoli in Notting Hill
Run by the Ruocco family since the 1980s, Da Maria is half-restaurant, half-shrine to the religion that is S.S.C. Napoli. Asides from the fact they screen games on match days, the real draw about this place is the inexpensive Italian family fare they serve, from fresh arancini to plentiful plates of parmigiana, pasta, pizza, polpette and pastiera. The memorable shopfront and mural add to the atmosphere, as does the fact Italians come from all over London to hang out at this veritable gem.
87 Notting Hill Gate, London W11 3JZ;
damaria.co.uk

⑮ Golborne Bistro
Much-loved local café-deli
For over 20 years, this spot has been a West London institution. There are few better ways to spend a sunny morning in Notting Hill than outside the Golborne Bistro for an al fresco brunch. Classics like cooked breakfasts and Eggs Benedict are excellent, as is their lunchtime sandwich offering and evening surf and turf menu. Afterward, you can peruse their deli, which stocks an impressive wine selection, fresh fruit & veg, and baked goods. At weekends, you will have to compete for a spot with the other punters, who come for the food and stay for the ambience.
100-102 Golborne Road, W10 5PS;
goldbournefinewinedeli.com

⑯ Jay Dees Catering
Jamaican food outlasting gentrification
If you can't get your jerk fix on carnival day, then just head down to Jay Dees at any time of the year, where you'll find Jamaican food at its finest. Predating the posh takeover of the area, this is authentic fare – think generous servings of curry mutton, fried chicken, smoked meats, rice & peas and coleslaw. Plantain, dumplings, fritters and patties can all be enjoyed too, and best of all it's all great value, thanks in part to it being takeaway only.
28 Lancaster Road, W11 1QP;
jaydeescatering.com

⑰ Lisboa Patisserie
Portuguese pastry shop famous for its pastel de nata
Lisboa Patisserie is legendary in London – it is the go-to destination for all manner of Portuguese products, but especially for pastel de nata. The iconic façade, with its 60s typeface and awning, greets you in a space that is functional formica, rather than cosy caff. That said, if you want to bag yourself a table or even a custard tart, arrive early because this is one of the most popular spots in the area. A Portuguese espresso or the Brazilian soft drink Guaraná Antarctica are the best way to wash down one of the sweet treats. If you can, take your time at this wonderful local institution, particularly on a market day, when you can sit with a coffee and watch the world go by.
57 Golborne Road, W10 5NR;
lisboa.co.uk

Outdoors

⓲ Holland Park
Kyoto meets Kensington in London's best Japanese garden

Holland Park is the largest green space in the well-heeled Royal Borough of Kensington and Chelsea and is surrounded by grand residential mansion houses. Central to the park are the murals and terraces that are the last remnants of Holland House, which was destroyed by bombing during WWII. The house was originally named after a former owner, the Earl of Holland, whose wife is said to have introduced the Dahlia to England. The site is now used as a venue for open-air theatre during the summer. Most people flock to the Japanese-style Kyoto Garden with its Koi-filled pond and waterfall. The sloping woodlands that surround it are good for spotting the fifty or so species of birds found here in the last decade. Peacocks roam by day, while long-eared bats dart around as dusk falls. The Ecology Centre in the stable yard has maps, nets for pond dipping and is a great source of wildlife information. There's also a great café and numerous sports facilities too.
Ilchester Place, W8 6LU;
rbkc.gov.uk/parks

⓳ Kensington Gardens
Royal garden at the edge of Hyde Park

Being one of London's posher neighbourhoods, most of Notting Hill's green space is in the form of private squares. But despair not, as just five minutes from Notting Hill Gate you'll find the tranquil Kensington Gardens. Originally part of Kensington Palace, these gardens were imagined by Queen Caroline in the 18th century with the help of designers Henry Wise and Charles Bridgeman. Luckily for us, it was made public by Queen Victoria in 1841 and has retained its more 'royal' formal and manicured appearance. Many of the monuments and attractions here are dedicated to Princess Diana, as the park and neighbouring palace were where she spent so much of her adult life. If you've got little ones to entertain, then the playground named after her is not to be missed with it's large pirate ship for them to enjoy. For those that don't want to grow up, the whimsical Peter Pan statue in the northeast corner of the gardens features a QR-code-activated 'phone call' with the character. From there, the Serpentine Bridge connects to Hyde Park where you'll find plenty more attractions including boats for hire, a lido and the Serpentine Gallery, which hosts regular exhibitions and an artist's pavilion in the summer months.
Orme Square Gate, W2 4RL;
royalparks.org.uk

Richmond

Unlike most of London's neighbourhoods, Richmond's story is less about development and more about how it has remained a leafy regal suburb for centuries. Henry VII built Richmond Palace and Charles I established Richmond Park as his hunting grounds and since that time the neighbourhood has always attracted the wealthy. In the 18th century exquisite Georgian terraces were built to house them, which you can still enjoy exploring today. Although spoilt for choice, definitely make a beeline for Richmond Park, as there is nothing quite like it in London. In truth, multiple visits are in order, although you can make a good stab at things via an unplanned meander through the meadows and woodland, with the deer as your company and several cafés for refuelling. The second port of call must be the river, for on a fine day few spots have a better atmosphere, and you can pick between boating activities, pub gardens and historic houses. You can also enjoy meandering back into the town's main shopping and restaurant area by way of Richmond Green, which has now become a place of pilgrimage for fans of the hit show Ted Lasso, replete with a fan shop selling memorabilia for the fictitious Richmond FC. Further afield is the UNESCO World Heritage Site of Kew Gardens, or else an exploration of the Thames Path and Petersham Meadows, that leads to the remarkable Petersham Nurseries. Whichever way you choose to explore Richmond, you're sure to enjoy its charming pedestrian lanes, independent shops and incredible green spaces.

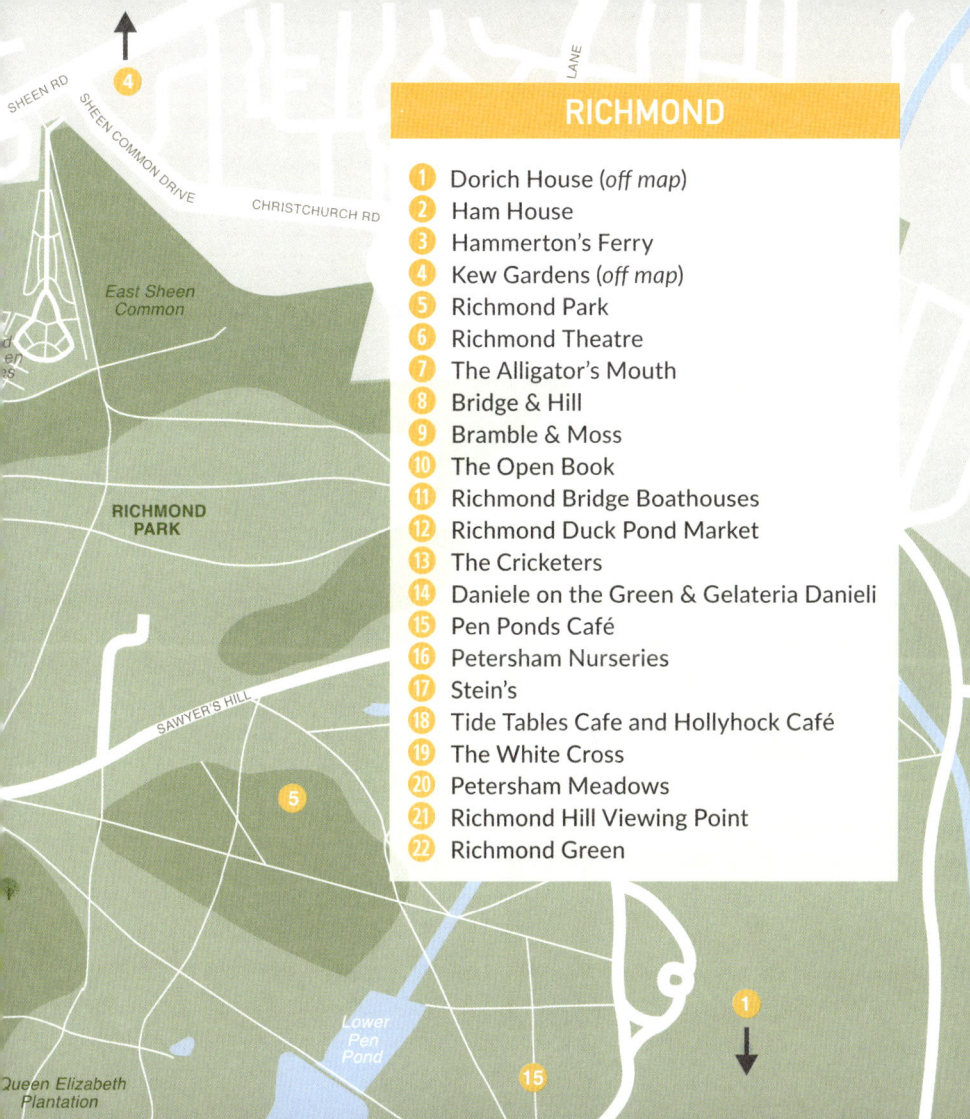

RICHMOND

1. Dorich House (*off map*)
2. Ham House
3. Hammerton's Ferry
4. Kew Gardens (*off map*)
5. Richmond Park
6. Richmond Theatre
7. The Alligator's Mouth
8. Bridge & Hill
9. Bramble & Moss
10. The Open Book
11. Richmond Bridge Boathouses
12. Richmond Duck Pond Market
13. The Cricketers
14. Daniele on the Green & Gelateria Danieli
15. Pen Ponds Café
16. Petersham Nurseries
17. Stein's
18. Tide Tables Cafe and Hollyhock Café
19. The White Cross
20. Petersham Meadows
21. Richmond Hill Viewing Point
22. Richmond Green

Richmond - Visit

Visit

❶ Dorich House
Home of sculptor Dora Gordine

A Modernist masterpiece, Dorich House was the studio and home of sculptor Dora Gordine and her husband, the diplomat-turned-collector Richard Hare. Designed by them in 1936, their estate was acquired by Kingston University after Gordine's death in 1991. A major restoration adapted the house for public use, returning it to its former splendour and filling the space with the sculptor's work, as well as Russian Imperial art amassed by the couple. Some dismissed the house as resembling a Soviet telephone box, but the brick exterior belies an elegant interior. Visitors first encounter a film about Gordine's life, before progressing to the studio spaces and sculptures. The modest top floor is the flat the couple occupied, where you can be a voyeur and imagine their lives through their belongings and the home they left behind.

67 Kingston Vale, SW15 3RN;
dorichhousemuseum.org.uk

❷ Ham House
A rare survivor of 17th-century luxury

Built in 1610 for a courtier of James I, and later extended by the Duke of Lauderdale, this fascinating historical site offers a glimpse into the lives of 17th-century England's wealthiest. The imposing, perfectly symmetrical south front of the building makes a bold statement about the power and taste of its occupants, while the opulent interiors are a testament to the extravagance of the era. Original elements are on display, like fine textiles, furniture, and paintings collected over 400 years ago. One of the highlights is the purpose-built library – a novelty at the time – and the wooden bathtub and bed in the bathroom. The gardens are perhaps the most glorious aspect, featuring a wilderness area, a terraced garden, formal lavender parterres, and intriguing outbuildings such as an ice-house, dairy and the earliest known still house. Visitors can also explore the walled kitchen garden, which supplies their café, the Orangery, with heritage food crops year-round. Audio guides and tours make for a more immersive experience, while regular ghost tours provide visitors with a chance to see if the Duchess of Lauderdale's ghost really does haunt the house.

Ham, Richmond, TW10 7RS;
nationaltrust.org.uk

❸ Hammerton's Ferry
Famous old ferry service that fought off the establishment

Hammerton's Ferry is a pedestrian and cycle ferry across the Thames, connecting Marble Hill House in Twickenham on the river's northern bank with Ham House on the southern bank. It is one of just four ferry routes in London that have not been replaced by a bridge or tunnel. Ferries have operated here since 1459 under the Tollemache family, who restricted public access, as portrayed in *Little Dorrit*. In 1908 resident Walter Hammerton began a regular service, much to the ire of the local lord. He challenged Hammerton, and thanks to much publicity and donations, managed to take the case to the House of Lords and win on appeal, this inspired a popular song at the time, 'The Ferry to Fairyland' (a nickname for Marble Hill House). After 38 years running the ferry, Hammerton retired and passed it on to Sandy Scott, who retained the company's royal warrant and has since passed it on to Hammerton's grandson, the musician Phil Collins. Today, weather permitting, the ferry operates on weekends year-round, and weekdays between March and October. Rowboats, canoes and motorboats can also be hired from the boathouse.

Marble Hill, Orleans Road, TW1 3BL;
hammertonsferry.com

❹ Kew Gardens
The world's largest, botanical collection

For two centuries, Kew Gardens has been an Eden for gardeners and researchers and is rightly a UNESCO World Heritage Site. This internationally renowned botanical garden is also one of London's most popular visitor attractions, with art spaces, educational resources, and year-round festivals like Kew the Music and Kew the Movies. Highlights include the Amazonian water lilies, the steamy Palm House, and the world's largest permanent orchid display. Kew's diverse landscapes range from rainforests to desert-like terrains and student allotments. The gardens hold about ten percent of the world's flowering plant species, from Chilean vine palms to giant metre-per-day bamboos, paralysing Strychnos trees and opium poppies. Kew even has its own police force to deter green-fingered thieves. The Pagoda offers panoramic views, while the aerial tree walk provides a lush forest canopy experience. Kew Palace allows you to see into the lives of King George III and Queen Charlotte, while the Marianne North Gallery houses over 800 vibrant plant paintings by the eponymous 19th-century artist. Exploring the vast grounds can be overwhelming, but the Kew Explorer land train offers a relaxed 35-minute tour.

Kew Gardens Road, TW9 3AE;
kew.org

⑤ Richmond Park
London's largest Royal Park

The largest of London's Royal Parks is also its most loved; the reason why becomes immediately apparent to anyone setting foot there. Situated on the edge of the city, Richmond Park feels far more like the countryside, not least owing to the population of red and fallow deer that have roamed the meadows and woodland here since Charles I opened it as his hunting grounds in 1637. But this Site of Special Scientific Interest and internationally significant nature reserve doubles as a sort of open-air gym, and on any given day you'll see hundreds of people making use of it for cross-country running, cycling, horse-riding and picnicking. There are rental bikes for those wishing to explore the surrounding paths, if you can navigate around the wandering deer or Lycra-clad racers. There is also a grassland area with rugby pitches and fishing ponds, as well as two eighteen-hole golf courses and riding stables. The central Isabella Plantation is a beautifully maintained woodland garden with a diverse range of plant life. It includes an enclosed playground, wooden bridges, streams, benches, and shaded grassy areas, providing a tranquil haven during the summer months. Several cafés are dotted around, most notably one at Pembroke Lodge – a Georgian mansion that was once the home of Lord John Russell and his grandson Bertrand Russell. For those seeking a more structured visit, the friends of Richmond Park organise free, monthly guided walks.

Richmond Park (Petersham Park Car Park Gate) TW10 5HU; royalparks.org.uk

⑥ Richmond Theatre
A great Victorian theatre

Built in 1899, Richmond Theatre is one of the finest surviving examples of the work of theatre architect Frank Matcham. Instantly recognisable with its red brick and buff terracotta, the building is now Grade II* listed. Despite being a suburban venue, it captivates audiences far beyond TW9 with its pre- and post-West End tours, that offer punters the chance of catching top-notch productions without the clamour of central London. Celebrity pantomimes over the Christmas holidays are always worth the ticket.

1 Little Green, TW9 1QH

Shop

❼ The Alligator's Mouth
Richmond's Children's bookshop
Named after a Lemony Snicket quote, this independent children's bookshop is a great place for kids to get lost in. With expert staff, regular events, author signings, postal subscriptions, various services for schools and biscuits on request, what more could you ask for? Nestled down a pedestrian backstreet close to Richmond Green, this makes for a magical detour when wandering Richmond. Well-behaved little ones can be rewarded with a scoop of Bakewell Tart ice cream from the nearby Willy Wonka-like gelateria.

2A Church Court, TW9 1JL;
thealligatorsmouth.co.uk

❽ Bridge & Hill
Homeware and Japanese design
Bridge & Hill Livingstore stands out as a rare find amid Richmond's chains. This independent shop offers a carefully curated selection of high-quality homeware, with a particular focus on Japanese goods, making it an ideal place to buy gifts. From ceramic donabe pots to glass terrariums, and Opinel knives aplenty, all products are thoughtfully chosen, and the expert staff enhance the entire experience. If you're looking for an alternative to mass-market goods available elsewhere, then Bridge & Hill should be your first port of call.

54 Hill Street, TW9 1TW;
bridgeandhill.com

❾ Bramble & Moss
Photogenic florist by Richmond Hill
Nestled behind a captivating shop front, Bramble & Moss is a top-notch independent florist. Their imaginative floral creations incorporate seasonal blooms along with unique elements like feathers and fruits. For whimsical and hassle-free home decor, their dried bouquets are perfect. Emphasizing the use of seasonal flowers, they expertly combine beloved British favourites like roses, peonies, and hydrangeas with uncommon ingredients, resulting in effortless beauty. With ample natural light flooding through the large glass exterior, Bramble & Moss is a delightful haven for flower enthusiasts.

64 Hill Rise, TW10 6UB;
brambleandmoss.co.uk

Richmond - Shop

❿ The Open Book
Richmond's best independent bookshop
Since 1987, The Open Book has been providing the book worms of Richmond with their drug of choice. The Tardis-like shop stretches back with shelves full of the best fiction and factual writing, as well as a selection of cards, wrapping paper and even rare books, should you be in search of a gift. They host occasional events, including book signings by local figures like David Attenborough. If you need a book ordered, they can source just about anything in print. If you're close to Richmond Green and in need of a browse, this charming independent is well worth a visit.
10 King Street, TW9 1ND

⓫ Richmond Bridge Boathouses & Boat Hire
Boats for sale & hire by this master builder
In case you're in the market for a traditional wooden Thames boat, look no further than the workshop of master boatbuilder Mark Edwards MBE. Or else, boat hire is an option for anyone looking to navigate the river at their own leisurely pace. Rowing skiffs for hourly hire to carry 1-8 persons are available throughout the season (March-October) on a first-come, first-served basis. All boats are supplied with life jackets if requested (compulsory for children). Rest assured, Mark and his company are boatbuilders with a royal pedigree – he was awarded his MBE by The Queen in 2015, having built barges for her Golden Jubilee.
Bridge Boathouses, TW9 1TH

⓬ Richmond Duck Pond Market
Thameside market for crafts & street food
Duck Pond run markets across London, but this one in Richmond is their most quaint, with 20-30 stalls operating over the weekend. Saturday is for street food, while Sunday showcases artisanal products, but you'll find a mix on both days. The square hosts several jewellers, local artists and companies selling their own designs, from handmade purses to photographs and lamps made from recycled scientific equipment. One textile artist makes fabric creations like masks, soft toys, cushions and bunting. There are also stalls specialising in vintage tableware and pet-themed gifts. Each week, the traders vary, but they all follow ethical and sustainable practices. The market offers a variety of street food, and is especially good for British fare like pies and sausage rolls. What's more, Heron Square provides a perfect scenic spot for a relaxing lunch with a view of the Thames.
Heron Square, Hill St, TW9 1EP

Eat

⑬ The Cricketers
Georgian pub on Richmond Green
This red-brick tavern dates from 1770 and overlooks Richmond Green, making it ideal for a sunny day when you can watch the amateur cricket at play, or else use it as a meet up point for before or after rugby matches at nearby Twickenham. The grub is good quality without descending into the pretensions of being a gastropub – think scotch eggs, fish and chips and sticky toffee puddings. During the summer the front is opened out onto the pavement with seating, although the old-world interior, adorned with all sorts of cricket artefacts, is the most agreeable place for a pint.
The Green, Richmond TW9 1LX

⑭ Daniele On the Green & Gelateria Danieli
Ice cream & Chocolate by Richmond Green
Daniele On the Green is one of the best places to source high-end chocolates in London. Wrapped in trademark blue boxes and sold from a picturesque shop by Richmond Green, it all has that Willy Wonka factor. Every flavour imaginable is available, including plant-based options. In the summer months the store also offers delicious ice cream, but this is the speciality of their sister shop, Gelateria Daniele, just a few doors down. Both stores are just by Richmond Green and a perfect place to take a break.
16 Brewers Lane & 13 The Green, TW9 1PX

⑮ Pen Ponds Café
Richmond Park pit stop en plein air
This is the refuelling spot of choice for locals, who return for the consistently great sausage or bacon sarnies, cappuccinos and pleasant atmosphere as people spread out on the benches nearby. Cakes, ice creams and other snacks are also available, as long as you don't mind things being a bit more homely than gourmet. Also bear in mind that opening times varying during autumn and winter depending on the closing time of the park, and on weekends things can sell out fast, particularly in the busy summer months.
Pen Ponds car park, Richmond Park, TW10 5HX

🟡 Petersham Nurseries
A pleasant café in a plant nursery
Petersham Nurseries is a Richmond-style restaurant through and through – a 'café' which feels as much like a florist, not least for the fact it doubles as a garden centre. Expect a bourgeois bohemian aesthetic with mismatched and worn wooden furnishings all inside a verdant greenhouse. They serve comforting Italian food like truffle tortellini, fresh ricotta salads and sorbets. The nurseries also feature a Tea House serving light lunches and cake, and a shop, offering the perfect respite for escapist urbanites.

Off Church Lane, Petersham Road, TW10 7AB

🟡 Stein's
A taste of Germany by the Thames
Richmond's riverside on a sunny day is a fascinating contrast. On one side, the crowded pubs leave no space to spare as people vie for a spot. On the other lies the serene expanse of the manicured meadows of Richmond Hill, perfect for picnics by the tranquil Thames. Venture a little further, however, and you'll find the sweet middle path, in the form of a beer garden called Stein's, offering refreshment like Adlerkonig and Erdinger. To accompany the cold beer, the menu offers delights like currywurst smothered in a sweet, tangy sauce and large schnitzels with potatoe salad. Stein's feels like a Munich beer garden and is popular with the large German community that have made Richmond their home.

Towpath, Petersham Road, TW10 6UX

🟡 Tide Tables & Hollyhock Café
Sister cafés with the best views in Richmond
These sister cafés in Richmond are charming spots to enjoy vegetarian food with a view. You can choose between looking onto the river from a large, tree-covered outdoor space and archway (Tide Tables), or in a rustic cottage surrounded by Terrace Gardens (Hollyhock Café). Both serve homely vegetarian and vegan food like pies, lasagne and salad, and only make use of fair trade, organic produce. If you just want a snack, they also have a range of beers, hot drinks and pastries. Prices are very fair, and the locations some of the best in Richmond.

Tide Tables: 2 The Arches, TW9 1TH
Hollyhock: 146 Petersham Road, TW10 6UX

🟡 The White Cross
Best place to be a cast-away
This Grade II listed boozer is a local favourite for lunch by the Thames, or in it if you're (un)lucky – the tide can go right up into the garden, and being marooned mid-pint makes for an especially amusing experience. Dog-friendly, with a huge garden and often showing the rugby, it's little wonder the crowds here on a sunny day fill up the otherwise spacious 18th-century building. And that's before you get to their quality Sunday roasts, bar snacks like beer-battered Cumberland sausages and oysters. During the summer, they offer paddle boarding experiences that depart right from the shores of the pub. There are few places more pleasurable to get stranded than the Cross.

Riverside House, Water Lane, TW9 1NR

Richmond - Eat & Drink

Richmond - Outdoors

Outdoors

⑳ Petersham Meadows
Former farmland by the river

Easily reached via the scenic Thames Path, Petersham Meadows feels a world away from London. A 24-acre expanse of meadowland complete with a herd of Belted Galloway cows in the summer and abundant plant diversity. It's the perfect place for nature lovers to escape the crowds and travel back in time to when the capital contained many more rural idylls like this. The meadow also leads on to Petersham Nurseries, should you be seeking something to eat after a day exploring this bucolic pocket of London.

River Lane, TW10 7AG

㉑ Richmond Hill Viewing Point
View protected by an Act of Parliament

Richmond Hill isn't just the road up to the royal park – it hides just as significant an attraction of its own. This scenic stretch runs parallel to the historic Thames meadowlands, providing visitors with an awe-inspiring view from the renowned Terrace Walk. Dating back to the 18th century, this picturesque promenade offers a vista of such acclaim that it has been safeguarded by its own Act of Parliament, ensuring its preservation for generations to come. To be captivated here is to be in good company, for the view has been painted by Turner, Reynolds and countless other artists.

130 Richmond Hill, TW10 6RN

㉒ Richmond Green
Urban oasis with a royal, sporting history

Pevsner described Richmond Green as 'one of the most beautiful urban greens surviving anywhere in England'. Surrounded by an eclectic mix of historic buildings, the Green has the languid quality of summer weekends spent picnicking, or watching cricket. The history of sport here dates back to the Middle Ages, when jousting tournaments and archery contests were held outside Henry VII's Richmond Palace, while cricket has been popular here since at least the 1700s. The Green's left flank contains the renowned terraces of Maids of Honour Row. These were built in 1724 for the maids of honour (trusted royal wardrobe servants) of Queen Caroline, the queen consort of George II. Meanwhile, Old Palace Lane, which has remnants of the royal residence, runs gently down to the river. Many of the surrounding buildings are Grade I-II* listed. The Green has two village cricket teams affiliated with nearby pubs, The Prince's Head and The Cricketers (see p.281), who play Twenty20 matches in the summer months.

The Green, TW9 1LX

Hammersmith & Chiswick

Hammersmith, and neighbouring Fulham and Chiswick, are especially ancient parts of London. Once the manor of the Bishops of London, the area has been the site of several significant settlements and skirmishes throughout history. But from the 19th century, infantry traded places with industry, as barges ferried goods from the factories and breweries that lined the riverbanks, most notably Fuller's, London's largest and oldest brewery. Hammersmith and Chiswick boast several houses of historically significant figures, particularly those from the Arts and Crafts movement. All are worth checking out – pick between Fulham Palace, the old digs of William Morris, Emery Walker or William Hogarth or the grandeur of Chiswick House. There are plenty of options for food, but the River Café is guaranteed to leave you with lasting memories. And best of all is just a lazy meander down the Thames Path, where you can take in the views and stop off for refreshments at one of the many historic pubs along the way.

Visit

❶ Chiswick House and Gardens
Neo-Palladian masterpiece

The final word in classical chic when it opened in 1729, Chiswick House remains a sumptuously stylish pad by any standards. Owner-architect Lord Burlington was inspired by the architecture of Ancient Rome and Renaissance architect Andrea Palladio. After completing the Grand Tour, Burlington returned home with 878 trunks of art acquisitions and set about designing a building that would represent the domestic, religious and civic elements of Roman architecture. The result is his masterpiece – a villa not intended as a residence but rather an art gallery and luxury party pad. The interior centres around the octagonal domed tribunal and includes the resplendent Red, Green and Blue Velvet Rooms. The latter was Burlington's study, whose royal blue and gold colour scheme make Lady Burlington's perfectly pleasant bed chamber look rather dowdy in comparison. A pair of original Chiswick tables designed by Burlington's artistic collaborator William Kent are among the treasures on display, along with a set of paintings of Chiswick House by Rysbrack. The historic gardens, also designed by Kent, are often described as the birthplace of the English landscape movement. The garden is a great place to explore and plays host the Duck Pond Market on Saturdays (see p.302).

Burlington Lane, W4 2RP;
chiswickhouseandgarden.org.uk

❷ Emery Walker's House
Authentic Arts and Crafts interior

Another famous house just down the road, Emery Walker was a friend of William Morris and likewise a leading proponent of the Arts and Crafts movement. However, his story is one of rags to riches – a working-class autodidact, by age 35 he established a company pioneering photogravure for book illustrations, that revolutionised bookmaking. This terraced house became his family home and was preserved by his daughter Dorothy and her nurse companion Elizabeth for posterity. The interior remains almost unchanged and is the only residence authentically adorned in the Arts and Crafts style. Like Kelmscott House, several notable figures occupied this Georgian (c. 1755) property before Walker, but the most impressive aspect of the building are the artefacts bequeathed by the engraver. They feature the only known example of a Morris linoleum still in its original domestic setting, as well as patterned wall-hangings and some of Walker's 'personal' belongings like his spectacles and a lock of his hair. Other items from Arts and Crafts proponents include all the possessions of architect Philip Webb (inherited upon his death), a secretaire designed by Ernest Barnsley and a teapot of Dante Gabriel Rossetti. Today, the Emery Walker Trust offer pre-booked guided tours and thanks to their work this exquisite time capsule is here for all to enjoy.

7 Hammersmith Terrace, W6 9TS;
emerywalker.org.uk

❸ Fulham Palace
Former home of the Bishops of London

Now a museum and garden, Fulham Palace is a part Tudor, part Georgian and part Victorian masterpiece that was once the rural retreat of the Bishops of London. They resided here for over 700 years, with the last Bishop leaving in 1975. The palace now educates about the site's history from prehistoric times through to Roman settlement up to the present. Although peaceful today, its past was hardly tranquil. Several inhabitants were murdered: Nicholas Ridley was burned at the stake in 1555, William Laud was beheaded in 1645, and the ghost of the bishop Bonner, who died in prison in 1569, is said to haunt the Tudor courtyard. More tangible exhibits are archaeological remains, a mummified rat and Bishop Winnington-Ingram's bejewelled mitre and cope. Benjamin West's pious depictions of Thomas à Becket and Margaret of Anjou are among the paintings on display. Fulham's bishops were keen gardeners whose horticultural legacy is evident in the 13-acre grounds. Here are rare trees, a recreated 19th-century knot garden and *The Bishops' Tree* by Andrew Frost, which depicts many of Fulham's prelates, carved into the trunk of a Cedar of Lebanon.

Bishops Avenue, SW6 6EA;
fulhampalace.org

❹ Hogarth's House
Family home of the father of British painting

With the less than tranquil pastures of the A4 and the roundabout bearing his name adjacent, it takes some imagination to see Hogarth's 'little country box by the Thames' as he must have. But this quaint 18th-century red brick, only one room deep, retains its charming original features, including a walled garden with a craggy old mulberry. Widely regarded as the father of British painting, Hogarth's fame now comes from his social observations and scathing moral commentaries in engravings like *The Rake's Progress*, *Marriage à la Mode* and *Gin Lane*, which are displayed throughout the house. Hogarth's interests were wide-ranging and as well as setting up an art academy and being responsible for the first copyright legislation, he was a philanthropist, instrumental in setting up the Foundling Hospital (see p.10). The family fostered several children and, in the summer, had foundling children stay with them in Chiswick, where they would eat mulberry pies.

Hogarth Lane, Great West Road, W4 2QN; hogarthshouse.org

❺ The Thames Path
London's loveliest walking path

Although you'd be hard-pressed to cover the 185-mile national trail that traces the Thames from its source near Kemble in Gloucestershire to Woolwich, the 6½ miles from Hammersmith Bridge to Richmond Bridge along the snaking banks of the river take in arguably the finest views in all of London. Along the way you'll pass notable sites like Fulham Palace, the Wetlands Centre at Barnes and Kew Gardens, as well as countless herons and many other worthy detours and distractions. Officially opened to the public in 1996, this route has long served navigation, with remnants of historic tolls still dotted along it, especially those dating from the Industrial Revolution and canal mania of the 18th and 19th centuries. These days you're much more likely to see people using the water for pleasure, whether rowing or sitting on the banks with a picnic. The entirety of the route is pedestrian and cycle friendly and takes around two hours by foot. With pubs and parks found intermittently along the way, you're never far from a place to rest and soak in this lovely stretch of the Thames. If you feel adventurous, you can extend the route beyond London's boundary or head east towards town. The proximity of tube stations at either end mean fatigued feet can be put to rest.

Hammersmith Bridge, W6 9DF

❻ William Morris Society, Kelmscott House
Resting place of Britain's foremost revivalist

While the William Morris Gallery in East London is better known (see p.169) – what that Walthamstow manor has in size, this smaller house makes up for in heritage. The Grade-II* listed Georgian mansion was built in 1785 and had several famous occupants before Morris, including Sir Francis Ronalds, who built the first electric telegraph in the garden, and George MacDonald, who wrote his magnum opus *The Princess and the Goblin* here in 1873. Morris settled here in 1878, changing its name from The Retreat to Kelmscott House in reference to Kelmscott, Oxfordshire, where he lived beforehand. It was here that Morris began printing and spent the last eighteen years of his life. Although part of the property remains private, the Society operates from the basement and coach house entrance, which is open to the public on Thursday and Saturday afternoons. Through talks, exhibitions and other events, the society helps explain the radical nature of Morris's work and its continued popularity today, with many of his designs still in production.

26 Upper Mall, W6 9TA

Eat & Drink

❼ Blue Anchor
Nautical pub with Thameside terrace

If following the Thames Path west from Hammersmith Bridge, the Blue Anchor is the first pub you'll see, and with that blue trim it's hard to miss. It's been there since 1722 and retained many period features, although along the way it has also collected an array of rowing artefacts. The pub has featured in the film *Sliding Doors* and the BBC drama *New Tricks*, but the real draw here is the good-quality pub fare and view of the water.

13 Lower Mall, W6 9DJ

❽ The Carpenters Arms
Backstreet gastropub with beautiful garden

The Carpenters Arms almost closed some years ago, but was rescued, stripped back to basics, and is now a local institution. In a square just off the Thames Path, it has a bright dining room, roaring fire and verdant garden, all of which make for the ultimate Sunday lunch setting. Originally opened in 1871, it later became a hangout for musicians from the neighbouring Island Records in the 70s. The pub retains some period features and it's approach to food is hearty and uncomplicated with an emphasis upon locally sourced ingredients. A great pub and one we hope will thrive for years to come.

91 Black Lion Lane, W6 9BG

Hammersmith & Chiswick - Eat & Drink

9 The Dove
Riverside pub with literary heritage
This stretch of the Thames is in no short supply of boozers, thanks to the several breweries that line the shore, but few have a history and vista like The Dove. A pub has existed here since the 17th century, and in that time has had quite the clientele. Charles II took his mistress here, James Thompson wrote *Rule, Britannia!* here in 1740, and other illustrious writers including Graham Greene, Ernest Hemingway, Dylan Thomas and the local William Morris, all favoured it for a pint. The front bar holds the Guinness World Record for the smallest public bar in the world too. Asides from Regency writers and pre-Raphaelites, a framed list of more recent renowned patrons hangs over the fireplace. The interior is cosy, with dark wood frames and furnishing, but the real highlight is the terrace, providing the perfect place to watch the world go by. As the pub is owned by Fullers, whose brewery is a stone's throw away, you can expect the pints on tap to be as fresh as can be.

19 Upper Mall, W6 9TA

10 The Elder Press Café
A perfect neighbourhood café
If in need of a picturesque pick-me-up setting, look no further. The Elder Press Café is a pastel-hued neighbourhood spot and is housed in a restored merchants building. Coffee, homemade pastries and brunch bits are all on offer, the latter costing around £10-£15. It's the kind of healthy fare you'd expect from a West London café, and is the best place to get your caffeine-fix before walking the Thames Path.

3 South Black Lion Lane, W6 9TJ

11 Patisserie Sante Anne
Pink Parisian patisserie by the park
Having relocated from Paris to Ravenscourt Park in 2014 after two decades of success there, Patisserie Sante Anne is one of the best places to get French baked goods in London. Using organic flour from Gloucestershire, Belgian chocolate and French butter for the croissants, the flavours are incredible and the execution flawless. Baguette sandwiches, éclairs, macaroons and tarte tatin, are all freshly prepared and very good value. What's more, the eye-catching pink façade and citrus interiors make for a welcome respite from the otherwise unassuming high street.

204 King St, London W6 0RA

⑫ The River Café
Tuscany-on-Thames
Restaurants are a fickle business and so few reach cult status, but the River Café is one of those that is as famous as its celebrity acolytes. Founded by the late Rose Gray and Ruth Rogers in 1987, it was originally the employee café of Richard Roger's architectural firm. A labour of love – he and his firm transformed an oil storage facility into a technicolour paean of Modernist design with a terrace by the Thames that is perfect in the summer months. Since the nineties, they've fed an especially star-studded crowd, and produced two stars of their own – Jamie Oliver and Hugh Fearnley-Whittingstall both sharpened their knives here. Thanks to its essentially unchanged approach to cooking – using as few, high-quality and in-season ingredients as necessary – it has retained a Michelin star since 1997. The café also produced several acclaimed cookbooks and TV programmes too. White peach bellinis, nettle pasta, all manner of veal and the infamous chocolate nemesis (which you must order) are some of the things that keep customers coming back for more. Aside from the eye-watering prices, the experience manages to be approachable whilst offering up something elegant and at times exquisite. If you're in need of somewhere for a special occasion, look no further.
Thames Wharf, Rainville Road, W6 9HA

⑬ The (other) River Café
Fulham's favourite dining establishment
Although it doesn't have a Michelin star or celebrity clientele like its namesake neighbour, this River Café is just as much of an Italian gem and part of London's food heritage. British food has been irrevocably shaped by the immigrants that opened caffs like this and who turned hearty breakfasts from a pastime of the privileged to a part of mass culture. Now, for many, few pleasures are as great as a greasy spoon breakfast in a traditional setting – Formica tables, tiled walls and kitsch pictures of the Adriatic. Three generations of the same Italian family have run the place since the sixties, and rightly have a loyal clientele coming for a Full English, bowl of 'spag bol', or custard-drenched apple crumble and hot cups of tea.
1A Station Approach, London SW6 3UH

Shop

⓮ Duck Pond Market Chiswick
Eclectic market in an atmospheric setting
This unique market takes place within the grounds of Chiswick House every other Saturday. One regular trader sells framed reproductions of great artworks and maps, starting from around £20. If you're looking for original work, potter Maria Murtagh sells her unique stoneware ceramics. There are several jewellers and textile stalls, as well as traders with candles, PJs, summer dresses and fun things for kids. Woven baskets make the whole affair more colourful, and with beauty products, you can always try before you buy. Dogs are welcome, not least because there are toys and treats for sale. Hungry humans will also find excellent street food.
Burlington Lane, W4 2RP

⓯ Foster Books
Rare shop for rare books
Housed in the oldest shop on the street, this 18th century bow-windowed building is the bookshop of your dreams and has been delighting locals and travellers for the last 50 years. They specialise in hard-to-find, out-of-print, used and rare books, so a visit is bound to be a treasure hunt and yield a find or two. The owners have a particularly strong eye for beautiful book covers, so if you're looking to spice up your shelf then Foster Books should be the first port of call.
183 Chiswick High Road, W4 2DR

⓰ The Old Cinema
Department store for vintage furniture
The last thing you'd expect in a cinema or the high street, The Old Cinema is a cornucopia of 20th-century collectables. The 19th-century converted building is the perfect location for an antique shop and there are also more recent items that have been given new life through their in-house expert upcycling. If you're after utilitarian storage, steel desks and sideboards straight out of a modernist apartment, you've come to the right place. You can also easily accessorise with old trunks, Anglepoise lamps or Eastern artefacts.
160 Chiswick High Road, W4 1PR

⓱ Wheelers of Turnham Green
Family-run florist and garden centre
Whether you're in the market for artistic wedding arrangements or a simpler shrub, the Wheeler family have you covered. Established by Spencer and Jason in 1993, they've been a go-to for bouquets, trees, containers and garden ornaments ever since, and now work alongside set designers for box-office Hollywood films like James Bond and Batman, as well as popular TV shows. If you're after advice before you buy, then they also offer workshops, landscaping and maintenance services.
Cato's Yard, Turnham Green Terrace, W4 1LR

OUTDOORS

ⓘ Bishops Park
Park beside the priestly palace
Under the shadow of Fulham Palace and Craven Cottage, Bishops Park is a Grade II* listed respite along the Thames. Open since 1893, it boasts playgrounds, meadows, a sculpture garden and 'urban beach'. The view of the river and Putney Bridge means it also offers the perfect vantage point for the annual Oxford vs. Cambridge boat race. You can still see some of the ancient parts of Fulham Palace's grounds, that contrast with newer features like a playground with fountains.
Bishop's Avenue, SW6 6EA

ⓘ Ravenscourt Park
Rival park to Fulham Palace
An ordered expanse of open land in a well-heeled area of London, Ravenscourt Park dates from 1888. When established, Ravenscourt House (at the Paddenswick Road entrance) provided a second residence for the Bishop of London. The building crumbled under bombing in 1941, and now a walled garden blossoms in its place. Neatly sculpted topiary, lively flowerbeds and serene communal seating are all beautifully arranged here, thanks to the local volunteers. In other areas of the main park, the prettiest spot is beside the tree-lined lake, best viewed from the humpbacked bridge. Children have a playground and paddling pools, and parents in need of refreshment can stop by at the Teahouse.
Ravenscourt Road, W6 0SL

ⓘ London Wetland Centre
West London's largest wildlife reserve
One of nine UK conservation centres run by the Wildfowl & Wetland Trust, the London Wetland Centre opened in 2000 and within two years earned itself a Site of Special Scientific Interest (SSSI) designation. The first project of its kind in the world, its 105 acres have been carved out in an area that's just four miles from central London. The centre gives its many visitors a chance to observe the growing populations of rare or threatened wildlife that thrive on the site's open water, lakes, mudflats and reedbeds. The whole area is dotted with various indoor and outdoor features including a 3-screen cinema that shows short films about the centre's work, and an art gallery displaying wildlife and landscape art. Other activities include tours and workshops, from bird feeding with a warden to wildlife photography. Near the edge of the lakes, the three-storey Peacock Tower provides panoramic views of the reserve and the expanse of marshland, where wildfowl like wigeon, lapwing and snipe regularly gather. There's also a pristine split-level heated bird observatory that gives views of the main lake and London skyline. The whole area is great for adventurous children, but there's also a playground with underground tunnels to enjoy.
Queen Elizabeth Walk, SW13 9WT

Hammersmith & Chiswick - Outdoors

Index

Symbols
2 Willow Road 65, 66, 68
14 Parish 210, 221

A
Abney Park Cafe 80, 92
Abney Park Cemetery 80, 82
The Alligator's Mouth 268, 276
Almeida Theatre 100, 102
Al Waha 250, 260
Andrew's Restaurant 6, 18
Angel Comedy @ Bill Murray 100, 102
Angel Delicatessen 100, 113
Argents and Rose 36
Arnold Circus 142, 160
Artwords 128, 129
ATIKA 144
Auld Shillelagh 80, 92

B
Backyard Market 144
Barbican Centre 47, 48, 50, 59
Barbican Conservatory 48, 60, 61
Bar Bruno 28, 41
Bar Italia 28, 41
Beigel Bake 140, 141, 144, 154
Beijing Dumpling 30
Bentham, Jeremy 6, 10
Beppe's Café 48, 56
Bermondsey Antique Market 186, 196
Bermondsey Beer Mile 185, 188, 189
Berwick Street 28, 36
Bishops Park 288, 304
Black Cultural Archive 209, 210, 212,
Blackhorse Beer Mile 164, 174
Blackhorse Lane Atelier 164, 170
Bloomsbury Farmers Market 6, 18
Bloomsbury Group 5
Blue Anchor 288, 296
BookMongers 210, 215
Books for Cooks 250, 256
Borough Kitchen 66, 72, 186, 196
Borough Market 185, 186, 190, 191, 202, 204
Bostock, Frank 82
Boundary Estate 159
Bowie, David 36, 209
Bramble & Moss 268, 276, 277
Brat 142, 155
Brawn 142, 156, 157
Brick Lane 141, 142, 144, 145
Bridge & Hill 268, 276
British Museum 5, 6, 8, 9, 25
Brixton Market 209, 219
Brixton Village Market 210, 215
Brixton Windmill 210, 212
Broadway Bookshop 122, 128, 129, 130
Broadway Market 122, 128-9
Brockwell Lido 210, 225
Brockwell Park 209, 210, 224, 225
Brunei Gallery SOAS 6, 9
Brunswick Centre 6, 14, 15, 17, 22

Brunswick Square Gardens 6, 22
Buen Ayre 129
Bühler + Co. 164, 174
Burberry Outlet 122, 130
Burgh House 65, 68
Burton, James 22, 25

C

Café Cecilia 122, 132
Café TPT 30
Camden Passage 100, 106
Camera Museum 6, 15
Canova Hall 210, 221
Carnaby Street 28, 36
Carpenters Arms, The 288, 296
Casbah Records 228, 236
Casse-Croute 186, 200
Castle Climbing Centre 80, 82
Chamberlin, Powell and Bon 47, 50
Chapel Market 100, 107
Charles Dickens Museum 6, 9
Charterhouse 47, 48, 50
Chinatown 27, 28, 30
Chiswick House 287, 288, 290, 302
Chris Bryant's Musical Instruments 36
Churchill Arms, The 250, 260
Church Street Bookshop 80, 86
Ciao Bella 6, 18
Circus Brixton 210, 216
Climpson & Sons 122, 132
Clissold Park 80, 96, 97
Clover's 210, 221

Cocktail Trading Co., The 142, 156
Columbia Road Market 142, 146, 147
Condor Cycles 6, 15
Coram, Thomas 10
Coram's Fields 5, 6, 22
Cow, The 249, 250, 260
Cricketers, The 268, 280, 281, 285
Culpeper Community Garden 100, 117
Curzon Bloomsbury 15
Cutty Sark 227, 228, 230

D

Da Maria 250, 263
Daniele on the Green 268, 281
Dark Sugars 144
Daunt Books 250, 256, 257
Denmark Street 28, 36
Denmark Street Guitars 36
Dennis Severs' House 142, 148
Design Museum 250, 252
Diverse Gifts 210, 216
Donlon Books 128, 129
Dorich House 268, 270, 271
Dove, The (Broadway Market) 129
Dove, The (Hammersmith) 288, 299
Druid Street 188, 189, 195, 204, 205
Duck Pond Market Chiswick 288, 302
Duke, The 6, 18,
Duke of Hamilton, The 66, 75
Duke of Edinburgh, The 210, 222
Dumplings' Legend 30

E

E5 Bakehouse 122, 133
Ebtd 164, 170
Effra Hall Tavern 210, 222
Elder Press Café 88, 299
Electric Avenue 210, 214, 215
Embassy Electrical Supplies 48, 55
Emery Walker's House 288, 290
Epitome 147
Epping Forest 163, 164, 179
Esters 80, 93
Estorick Collection 100, 102
Etles 164, 174
Every Space, The 164, 170

F

Fabrications 129
Fan Museum, The 228, 230
FARA Charity Shop 100, 108
Fashion & Textile Museum 185, 186, 192
Fawkes, Keith 72
First Stop Café 172
Fish Wings & Tings 210, 223
Flashback Records 100, 108
Flask Walk 66, 72
Flea London Vinegar Yard 186, 196
Fortune Street Park 48, 56, 59, 61
Foster Books 288, 302
Foundling Hospital 10, 22, 293
Foundling Museum 6, 10
Four Corner Chess Club 48, 50
Four Hundred Rabbits 210, 223
Four Seasons 30
Foyles Bookshop 28, 38
Franca Manca 129
French House, The 28, 41
French Protestant Church of London 44
Frizzante Café 160
Fulham Palace 287, 288, 292, 295, 304

G

Garcia's Deli 249, 250, 257, 259
Gelateria Danieli 268, 281
Get Stuffed 100, 108
Giacobazzi's 66, 75
Giddy Up Coffee 48, 56
Ginger & White 66, 75
Goddards at Greenwich 228, 240, 241
God's Own Junkyard 163, 164, 166
Golborne Bistro 250, 262, 263
Golden Heart, The 142, 156
Goldfinger, Ernö 68
Good Friend Chicken 30
Goodhood 142, 150
Gordon Square 6, 22
Gosh! Comics 36
Grant Museum of Zoology 6, 10
Greenwich Market 228, 236, 241
Greenwich Market Food Hall 228, 241
Greenwich Park 228, 234, 241, 242, 245
Growing Communities' Market 80, 86

H

Hackney City Farm 142, 160, 161
Hackney Empire 122, 124

Hackney Flea Market 80, 86
Hackney Museum 122, 124
Ham House 268, 270, 271, 272
Hammerton's Ferry 268, 272
Hampstead Community Market 66, 72
Hampstead Jazz Club 75
Harry Brand 147
Haygen 100, 108, 109
Hay's Galleria 186, 198
Heap's Gourmet Sausages 228, 241
Heath, The 65, 66, 71, 72, 76
Herne Hill Books 210, 216
Herne Hill Market 210, 215
Hertford Union Canal 137
Highbury Fields 100, 117
Hill & Szrok 122, 133
Hiroshima Tree 25
Hirst, Damien 42, 53, 195
Hogarth's House 288, 293
Holland Park 249, 250, 256, 264
Hollyhock Café 268, 282
House of St Barnabas 44
Hub Café, The 138

I

Indian Veg 100, 113
International Magic Shop 48, 54, 55
Island Queen, The 100, 113
Islington Green 100, 116, 117
Isokon Gallery 66, 68, 69

J

Jay Dees Catering 250, 263
Judy Green's Garden Store 72
Junk Shop, The 228, 238, 239

K

Keats, John 71
Keats House 66, 71
Kelmscott House 288, 290, 295
Kensington Gardens 250, 264
Kenwood House 66, 71, 76
Kew Gardens 267, 268, 272, 273, 295
Kingly Court 36
King's Head 100, 112, 113
Kitchen Provisions 80, 87
Know & Love 80, 88
Kowloon Bakery 30
Koya Ko Hackney 122, 134, 135
Krypton Komics 162, 170

L

Labour and Wait 142, 150
La Crêperie de Hampstead 66, 75
Lamb, The 6, 21
Lambeth Country Show 225
Last Tuesday Society, The 122, 127
Lauriston Village 122, 131
Leathermarket Gardens 186, 207
L'eau a La Bouche 128, 129
Lee's Sea Food 147
Leighton House 249, 250, 252
Leila's 142, 159, 160

Levison's Vintage Clothing 144
Liberty 28, 38
Libreria Bookshop 142, 151
Lisboa Patisserie 249, 250, 263
Lloyd Park 163, 164, 169, 174, 177, 179
London Fields 121, 122, 127, 128, 133, 134, 136, 137
London Fields Lido 122, 124, 125
London Glassblowing 186, 198
London Review Bookshop 6, 15
London Tea Exchange 144
London Wetland Centre 288, 304
L & R Bookshop 250, 257
L. Terroni & Sons 48, 56
Lychee One 122, 124

M

MacColl, Kirsty 44
Made in Portugal 164, 177
Magazzino 186, 204
magCulture 48, 54, 55
Maison Bertaux 28, 42
Maltby Street Market 185, 186, 189, 202, 203
Marianne North Gallery 272
Market Porter, The 186, 190, 204
Market Row 215
Marksman Public House 144, 159
Marx, Karl 42
Meat N16 80, 87ß
M. Manze 185, 186, 200

Morris, William 38, 163, 164, 169, 287, 288, 290, 295
MOTH Club 122, 127
Mr Allsorts 100, 110, 111
Museum of Brands 250, 255
Museum of the Home 142, 148, 149
Museum of the Order of St John 48, 52

N

Naked Coffee 228, 239, 242
National Gallery, The 27, 28, 30
National Maritime Museum 228, 233
Netil House 122, 127
New River Path 99, 100, 117
Noble Rot 6, 21
Notting Hill Carnival 249

O

Old Cinema, The 288, 302
Old Operating Theatre 185, 186, 192
Old Royal Naval College 227, 228, 232, 233, 245
Old Truman Brewery 151
OMBRA 122, 134
One Scoop Store 80, 88-89
Open Book, The 268, 279
Otto's 6, 21
Oxfam 66, 72

P

Padella 114, 186, 205
Paper Dress Vintage 122, 131
Past Caring 100, 111

Patisserie Sante Anne 288, 299
Pavilion Bakery 129
Pavilion Café (Greenwich) 228, 242
Pavilion Café (Hackney) 138
Pembroke Lodge 275
Pen Ponds Café 268, 281
Pentreath and Hall 6, 16
Peter Harrison Planetarium 228, 235
Petersham Meadows 267, 268, 285
Petersham Nurseries 267, 268, 282, 284, 285
Phoenix Garden 28, 44
Phonica 36
Photographers' Gallery 28, 33
Pierrepont Arcade 106
Pierre Victoire 28, 42
pockets 122, 134, 135
Poppies 156
Portland Road 250, 259
Portobello Road Market 106, 249, 250, 258, 259
Postman's Park 47, 48, 61
Potter's Field Park 186, 207
Present & Correct 6, 16
Pride of Spitalfields 144
Primeur 80, 93
Prince Charles Cinema 28, 33
Prince of Greenwich, The 228, 242
Prince's Head, The 285
Pure Vinyl Records 210, 216

Q
Queen's House 228, 234
Quo Vadis 28, 42

R
Rachel & Malika's 210, 219
Ranger's House 228, 234
Rasa 80, 95
Ravenscourt Park 288, 304
Ravenswood Industrial Estate 164, 166
Ray-Stitch 100, 111
Reckless Records 36
Red Imp Comedy Club 164, 166
Regent's Canal 121, 137
Regent Sounds 36
Reliance Arcade 215
Retro Hub 80, 90-91
Retrouve 128, 129
Rich Mix 142, 148
Richmond Bridge Boathouses 268, 279
Richmond Duck Pond Market 268, 279
Richmond Green 279, 281, 285
Richmond Hill Viewing Point 268, 285
Richmond Park 267, 268, 275, 281
Richmond Theatre 268, 275
Rinse Showroom 144
River Café 287, 288, 301
Riverside Bookshop 186, 198
Rochelle Canteen 142, 158, 159
Ronnie Scott's 27, 28, 34
Rough Trade 142, 151

Royal Hill 228, 239, 242
Royal Observatory 227, 228, 235
Russell Square 6, 25

S

Sadler's Wells Theatre 100, 102, 103
Saint Patrick's Catholic Church 44
Sambourne House 250, 255
Saponara Pizzeria 100, 114
Sayeh & Galton Flowers 72
Scoop Amphitheatre 184, 207
Scotti's Snack Bar 48, 56
SCP 142, 152
Screen on the Green 100, 104
Shakespeare's Globe 185
Shard, The 185, 186, 194
Sister Ray 36
Skoob Books 6, 17
Sloe Vintage 210, 219
Smithfield Market 48, 53
Soho Square 27, 28, 44
Soho Theatre, Walthamstow 162, 166
Somewhere in Hackney 122, 131
Sonora Taqueria 80, 94, 95
Sounds of the Universe 36
Southwark Cathedral 185
SPACE 122, 127
Spitalfields Market 142, 147
St Bartholomew the Great 48, 53
Stein's 268, 282
St George's Gardens 6, 22
St JOHN 47, 48, 58, 59
St John Bakery 185, 205
St Mary's Old & New Church 80, 85
Stoke Newington Bookshop 80, 91
Stoke Newington Car Boot Sale 80, 91
Sublime 131
Supertone Records 210, 218, 219
Sushi Show 100, 114, 115
Sway Gallery Japanese Store 48, 55

T

Tavistock Square 6, 17, 25
Thames Clipper boat 227
Thames Path 267, 285, 287, 288, 295, 296, 299
Theatreland 34
Theatre Pubs 100, 104
Tide Tables Café 268, 282
Today Bread 162, 177
Tofu Vegan 100, 114
Token Studio 186, 195
Trafalgar Tavern 228, 242, 243
Trullo 100, 115, 116
Two Columbia Road 142, 152, 153

U

Unicorn Theatre 186, 195
Union Chapel 100, 105
The Upmarket 144

V

Vestry House Museum 169
Vicoli Di Napoli Pizzeria 80, 95
Victoria Miro 100, 105

Victoria Park 122, 138, 139
Victoria Park Market 122, 134, 135
Vintage Market 144

W

Walthamstow Market 163, 164, 172, 173
Walthamstow Village 162, 169
Walthamstow Wetlands 163, 164, 180
Waterstones 6, 17, 38
Watts, G.W. 61
Wellcome Trust & Collection, The 6, 12, 13
The West End 27, 28, 33, 34
Wheelers of Turnham Green 288, 302
The White Cross 268, 282
Whitecross Street Market 48, 59
White Cube 185, 186, 195
William Morris Gallery 163, 164, 169, 174, 177, 179
William Morris Society 288, 295
Wong Kei 30
Woodberry Wetlands 80, 85
Wood Street Indoor Market 162, 173
Virginia Woolf 25, 42

Y

Ye Olde Mitre 48, 59
Yield N16 80, 91

Image credits:
p.11 Jeremy Bentham auto icon © UCL Institute, p.12 & p.13 © the Wellcome Trust, p.16 © Pentreath & Hall, p13 © Present & Correct, p.19 The Duke © pubgallery.co.uk, p.20 © Noble Rot, p.21 Otto's © Nic Crilly- Hargrave, p.32 © The Prince Charles Cinema, p.39 © Liberty, p.54 © magCulture, p.58 ST JOHN © Stefan Johnson, p.68 © Willow Road, p.69 ©TDK Isokon Gallery, p.70 © English Heritage, p.74 © Ginger & White, p.83 © Castle Climbing Centre, p.92 © Auld Shilleagh, p.93 Esters ©Jonathan Simpson, p.103 Sadler's Wells © Philip Vile, p.112 © The King's Head, p.149 Museum of the Home (top) © Jayne Lloyd, (bottom left) © Em Fitzgerald, (bottom right) © Hufton & Crow, p.150 © Labour and Wait, p.151 Libreria Bookshop © Iwan Baan, p.155 © Brat, p.157 Brawn © John Carey, p.158 Rochelle Kitchen © Anton Rodriguez, p.162 & p.167 © God's Own Junkyard, p.171 © Blackhorse Lane Atelier, p.180 & p.181© London Wildlife Trust, p.192 © Old Operating Theatre , p.193 © Fashion Textile Museum, p.201 © Manze, p.204 © Padella, p.223 Fish Wings & Tings / Veg & Tings © Nic Crilly- Hargrave, p.231 © Cutty Sark, p.232, p. 232 Painted Hall © Nikhalesh Haval, p.234 © Queen's House, p.235 Royal Observatory © Chris Dorney, p.252 Leighton House © Dirk Lindner, p.254 Sambourne House © Jaron James, p.261 © Churchill Arms, p.291 Chiswick House © Anna Kunst, p.292 © Fulham Palace, p.293 © Hogarth House, p298 © The Elder Press Cafe, p.300 River Café © Matthew Donaldson, p.303 © The Old Cinema, p.305, p.303 London Wetland Centre © Martyn Pyner, (bottom right) © Robert Chadwick.

About us:

Metro is a small independent publishing company with a reputation for producing well-researched and beautifully-designed guides. To find out more about Metro and order our guides, take a look at our website: **www.metropublications.com**